The nomadpreneur author of Turn Your Passion into Profit presents

Living True to Your Self!

Reclaim your power! Break Free! Live your dream!

Walt F.J. Goodridge

Living True To Your Self

© Walt F.J. Goodridge. All rights reserved.

This book may not be reproduced in whole or in part, or transmitted in any form, without written permission from the author and publisher, except by a reviewer who may quote brief passages in a review.
Contact: walt@waltgoodridge.com

Published by
a company called W
Paperback Retail Cost: $16.00; 220pp
Paperback ISBN-13: 978-0-9835808-1-2(AMAZ)

Visit a store called W

Books, apps, audio, video, merchandise, courses, passion projects, freebies and more from a company called W!
www.waltgoodridge.com/store

Distributed exclusively by
The Passion Profit Company
(646) 481-4238
www.PassionProfit.com
sales@passionprofit.com

Educational institutions, government agencies, libraries and corporations are invited to inquire about quantity discounts.
Contact: sales@passionprofit.com

Printed in the United States of America

Note: The headings and some text are intentionally right justified. You are free to speculate as to why.
(walt@waltgoodridge.com)

Contents

A few quotes
Acknowledgments
Credits
A word about self
Once Upon a Time…
How to teach how
How it all began

13   Part ONE: PRELUDE & PAYOFF
These are some preliminary ideas
Living True Test #1: How to know if you are living true to your self
Living True Test #2: How to know if you've got what it takes
Living True Test #3: How to know if you've got the right priorities
Living True 101 (Student Edition)
Why aren't YOU living true?
A screenplay called YOU
A preview of things to come
You get to choose

31   Part TWO: PRELIMINARIES
This is how I define the concept
How I define living true to MY self
Word by Word
What is LIVING?
What is TRUE?
Bonus: Once we know the truth
What is the SELF?
In all areas of my life
Living true in the service of other selves
Putting it all together
Solving for happiness
Applying the key

83   Part THREE: PROS & CONS
Here's what to expect as you embark on your own journey
The Pros
The Cons
Bonus: The Tao of Shawshank

103   Part FOUR: PREREQUISITE
These are the things I believe about my self, about the world, about others and about the universe that help me to live true
Why you need a better belief system
Everything you believe…is wrong!
Seeing beyond the constructs
Criteria for a belief system
A Better Belief System:
The Universe is perfect
People are predictable
There is an unseen Realm
Part FOUR "B": PERSONALLY
About My Self
About Other People
About the Universe

155   Part FIVE: PERSONALITY
These are the qualities, attributes and personality traits that help me live true to my self.
The Personality Traits

169   Part SIX: PROMPTINGS
These are the things that I consciously I say to my self that help me live true
Self talk
What I say to my self
What I DON'T say to my self

179   Part SEVEN: PROCESS
These are the actual strategies I use to live true to my self
What I do
My Overall Strategy

199   a FINAL WORD
Harnessing my neuroses
The bigger picture

205   MY GUARANTEE
206   APPENDIX
215   OTHER BOOKS FROM WALT
216   ABOUT THE AUTHOR

A few quotes ▲

"Success in any endeavor depends on the degree to which it is an expression of your true self." ~ Ralph Marston

"It is impossible to help another being directly. It is only possible to make [a] catalyst available in whatever form. We cannot offer short cuts to enlightenment. It can only be accomplished by the self, for the self. Another self cannot teach enlightenment, but only teach information, inspiration, or a sharing of love, of mystery, of the unknown that makes the other-self reach out and begin the seeking process."
~ The Ra Material (B1, 161-162)

"There is the presumption here that you are willing to question the things you've always believed to be true and to consider that things are not always as they appear, no matter how entrenched in our societal norms they may be at present."
~ *The Great Sheep Uprising*, an unpublished manuscript.

Acknowledgments

I wish to thank Thelma Rose Goodridge, for making me who I am,
Sasha Poznyak (for giving me the idea for this book),
Christine Karmo, Randy Hyde, Pramod Khanna, Ken McRae, Ernest Capers, Dr. Heru Shango, Zelda Samara Owens, Nicole Drew, Diamond Davis, Tony Cordoza, Monica Afesi, Stacey Spencer-Willoughby, Howard Walters, Aaron Willoughby, Wayne Wright, Gurdeep Singh, Delxino Wilson de Briano, Joe Hill, Catherine Young, Ashley Moffatt, Jayvee Vallejera, Chun Yu Wang, Ron McFarlane, and Preeyaporn P. Jompeang
who have all, in significant ways, helped me live true to my self.

Credits

Cover image: "Beyond the Boxes" by Tony Cordoza (www.tonycordoza.com)

A word about self

You'll notice throughout this book, except where I'm quoting others (and selectively in the back cover copy), that I've separated the word *myself* into *my* and *self*. Similarly, *your self, her self, the self,* and the admittedly awkward-sounding *his self,* are used throughout. This separation was done in order to achieve just that—a separation—a redefinition, by providing a cognitively jarring challenge to how you think about, read, as well as speak about "self," as a an earthly manifestation distinct from who you really are.

So, while the title may thus be a bit confusing, the *self* to which I suggest you should strive to live true is the self that is most often suppressed by society, the self you chose and intended to manifest *before* the education, training, career advice, religion, and expectations of others, as well as society's lies covered it up and pushed it deep down. The goal of this book, therefore, is to help you find, resurrect, free, redefine, reinvent and transform your current self into a self that is the true and best reflection of the real YOU.

Once Upon a Time

Once upon a time, there was an unhappy civil engineer living in New York, who hated his job. More than anything else, he simply wanted the freedom to live true to his self. So, he followed his passion, started a series of sideline businesses, made enough money to quit his job, escaped the rat race, ran off to a tropical island in the Pacific, and created a tourism business so he could give tours of the island to pretty ladies every day and see the world. He now lives his happily reinvented, dream life as a "nomadpreneur" somewhere in a land far, far away.

"How," it all began

"How did you do it?"
"Well, I wrote my resignation letter, I walked it into my boss' office and I walked away from my job."
"No, I mean HOW did you do it?"
"I just told you."
"You told me WHAT you did, but I want to know HOW you did it, so I can do it too!"

My name is Walt F.J. Goodridge. I wrote this book because someone asked me a question I couldn't answer.

The question, as you've just read, had to do with *how* I was able to re-write my life story. That story—my story—is essentially a simple one: I was once a civil engineer. I hated my job. I started a sideline business and turned my passion into profit. I quit my job, ran away to live on a tropical island, and now live a nomadpreneur's life generating passive income while I roam the world. In other words, I reinvented my self so that I could live true to my self.

In the process of that reinvention, I wrote many books, including a popular book entitled *Turn Your Passion Into Profit*. I do workshops to help people discover their passions and turn them into profitable businesses. I am also the author of *Jamaican in China*!—a blog that chronicles my nomadpreneur adventures with the underlying goal of inspiring others to follow their own dreams.

Not being able to answer that question, therefore, presented a unique challenge, because answering questions and sharing knowledge and information is in integral part of what I do as part of my reinvented identity. In fact, the personal mission statement I've adopted for my life is *"I share what I know, so that others may grow."*

So, in what became a determined effort to develop a useful answer to the question, I realized that when it comes to living true to one's self, *how* is, in fact, a very difficult concept to communicate. I realized there is an inherent difficulty in teaching someone how to do something that is an entirely personal and subjective experience, and I was forced to think about things in a much different and deeper way.

The first question I had to answer was, *"How does one teach how?"*

How to teach how

"I am going to teach you how to live true to your self; first, you must do this..."

What's wrong with the statement above? The answer is, it contains an inherent contradiction.* The contradiction is that I cannot *teach* you how to live true to your self. It is something that can only be learned by your own personal experience.

It doesn't matter whether you're teaching someone how to sew, how to cook, how to play golf, ride a bicycle or play a sport. Most learning, other than the rote recitation and regurgitation of facts, requires experiential learning. In other words, one must experience it one's self in order to learn and master. The driving analogy works well here because of the similarity in concept to how we think about our lives. In life we often feel we are steering our lives forward towards a desired destination, sometimes alone, sometimes with companions and passengers. Also in life, we follow rules, we have the ability to change or reverse our direction, change destinations, go faster or slower, apply the brakes, and so on.

Teaching someone how to live life true to her self is similar to teaching someone how to drive a car in this regard: You can tell her <u>what</u> you do. You can show her how <u>you</u> do it. You can give her the rules of the road, and a few tips for how to do certain things, but the essence of driving, the actual learning of the skill, takes place once *the person you are teaching* takes the wheel and begins driving for her self.

Similarly, if you are the person doing the learning, you can *listen* to how I drive, you can *watch* me drive, and you can take written tests and quizzes on driving, but ultimately, in order for you to really understand driving and learn how to drive, you have to do it for your self—get behind the steering wheel, buckle up, put the car in gear, step on the gas and lurch

English majors are free to have fun deciding if this is indeed a "paradox," a "contradiction," a "self-refuting idea" or all of the above!—Walt

forward awkwardly, brake too harshly at first, lose control every now and then, make the mistakes most people do, acquire the feel, take a break, sleep on it, do it again the next day, and ultimately, over time, develop the skill in a hands-on, *experiential* manner. There is no shortcut or substitute for it.

There is also no shortcut or substitute for the personal experience required to live true to your self. Since one can only learn how by doing it, the only way to learn how to live true to the self is to get behind the wheel, so to speak—the wheel of one's own life—and to begin steering it in the desired direction and towards the desired destination.

However—and herein lies the inherent contradiction—since each "self" and thus each direction and destination is different for each person, then the experience, and thus the learning, as well as what is actually learned, is going to be different for each and every person. It might be essentially impossible, therefore, for me to even demonstrate how to live true to your self. That might be like teaching you how to be a baker, by demonstrating how to be a candlestick maker.

But, wait. All is not lost. I believe there *is* something I *can* do that may be extremely valuable. Since I can only demonstrate how *I* have lived, and continue to live true to *my* self, I can relate what I have done with a bit of a unique twist.

Simply sharing what I did—a list of steps or a set of actions—is not enough. However, it stands to reason that *what* I did is a function of who I am, of what drives me, what I believe, how I think, what I say and what I do. Therefore, if I could get *behind and inside* that identity, those private motivations, those beliefs, those words, and those actions, and actually deconstruct my concept of self, the rewards and payoffs that drive me, my belief system, my thoughts, my history, my self-talk, my observations, my analyses, my conclusions, and offer them with sufficient detail and nuance, then perhaps, I might succeed in offering what might approach a valuable demonstration of a life lived true to self. Only then could I really answer the question *How did you do it?*

Therefore, that's what this book will attempt to do. I will share all of those things mentioned to the best of my ability and recollection, with the intention and hope you might be able to extrapolate what I've shared to the extremely personal and private pursuit of living true to *your* self.

This book, therefore, can never really be a "how to" manual, it can only be a "how I do it" manual (Consider it a "prequel" to *Turn Your Passion Into Profit*). However, I think you will find this useful, because despite our individual uniqueness, there are some things we share in common.

When it comes to driving, however different the details of our individual journeys (choice of vehicle, route, speed, destination, etc.), we do share common dreams of how we want to *feel* once we get there. I will, therefore, share with you *my* desired direction and destination, how I learned to drive, what drives *me*, what I think about while I drive, how I steer, how I make my decisions, and how I, too, want to feel once I get there (because the journey never ends).

And as you begin to gather momentum and cover ground in your own journey, perhaps just like driving a car, with the wind in your face, in the company of loved ones, all moving in the same direction, enjoying the scenery together, you may find the joy is, in fact, in the getting there. Perhaps we'll both discover that in living true to your self, just as in driving, the journey is often what it's all about!

Road trip, anyone?!

Note: Even though this ISN'T a how to book, and I AM speaking about my personal experience, there is a certain amount of generalizing that you expect from someone you've paid to teach you how to drive. Well, you'll find those sprinkled throughout the book, and particularly in my Living Truisms. Speaking of which....

> **Living Truism:** Everyone seeks a unique experience of living, perceives a unique experience of truth, and operates from a unique experience of the self. Living true to the self, therefore, is ultimately a private experience that can only be learned through one's personal experience.

How we shall proceed

In deciding what to include in this book, my focus often wavered between offering the exhaustive or the essential—the minutiae or the main points. Let me explain.

As I said earlier, if living true to my self is a function of what I believe, then it must also be a function of what I *do not* believe. If it is a function of what I say to my self, then it must also be a function of what I *do not* say. Similarly, it must be influenced as much by what I do, as what I *don't do*.

See what I mean? Making an exhaustive list of what I believe, *and* what I *do not* believe is an impossible task. It would mean, essentially, dividing the thoughts and beliefs contained in every other book that has ever been written into two categories: those I believe, and those I don't. So, I must necessarily focus only on those things that I believe are the essential components and essential omissions of my thoughts, beliefs, self-talk and actions, and hope that I don't include too much that is irrelevant, or omit anything that is essential. (As you'll discover about my belief system, however, I believe this book is divinely inspired and guided, so I don't worry really too much about that, nor should you!)

With that said, I've divided this book into seven parts.

PART 1: These are some preliminary ideas to get us on the same page, assess where life is, and set some goals.

PART 2: This is how I define living true to my self.

PART 3: These are some of the challenges one might experience while living true to one's self.

PART 4: This is what I believe about my self, about people, about the world, and about the universe that help me live true.

PART 5: These are the qualities, attributes and personality traits I believe help me live true to my self.

PART 6: These are the things I consciously say to my self to move my self to action and live true.

PART 7: These are the actions, habits and behavior I exhibit that help me live true to my self.

Part ONE
PRELUDE &
PAYOFF

*"To be yourself in a world
that is constantly trying
to make you something else
is the greatest accomplishment."*
~ Ralph Waldo Emerson

The Living True Test #1

How to know if you are living true to your self

When asked, many people believe they are already living true to their selves. Here is a test to determine if you are.

1. Have you identified your purpose in life?

2. Are you in control of how you spend your time?

3. Are you actively spending your time engaged activities that help you fulfill your purpose?

4. Are you involved in any activities that are at odds with your ethics simply for survival or a paycheck? (Are you buying, selling, making, marketing or otherwise endorsing the buying, selling, making or marketing of goods and services or lifestyles that are at odds with your values or ethics?)

5. Are you involved in any relationships that are at odds with your ethics simply for survival or a paycheck?

6. Are you living in the location and lifestyle of your happiness?

In the broadest, general terms, living true to the self means, as a friend of mine was fond of saying, *"displaying the appropriate and healthy level of self-advocacy."* In other words, I, as my own advocate, must strive at all times to think, speak, be and behave in ways that support my physical, mental and spiritual survival, growth, and prosperity without infringing on the same of others. It means being in control of and steering my life towards the fulfillment of my purpose. It means engaging in a profession that serves my purpose. It means getting out of unhealthy relationships even if children are involved. It means living where and how I wish to live.

> **Living Truism**: In order to live true to your self, you must be in control of your life.

The Living True Test #2

How to know if you've got what it takes

Without a doubt, the essential qualities required to live true to your self are discipline and persistence.

Discipline

TEST EXERCISE:
(1) Find something you are addicted to.
(2) Willingly deprive your self of it for 10, 20 or 30 days.

If you do not have the discipline to delay gratification, postpone your pleasures, or resist temptation in the presence of, and with free access to the thing you crave, then you are simply not ready to live true to your self. You cannot live free if you are addicted.

For many people, food is such an addiction. A simple seven or ten-day water fast would prove if you've got what it takes. Other indulgences to consider abstaining from include cigarettes, sex, alcohol and television. But it isn't only vices. Sometimes it takes tremendous discipline to refrain from *positive* indulgences that are not in your best interest. For instance, some people are addicted to rescuing others, or doing for others at the expense of their own happiness. For them, the greatest show of discipline might be to resist the urge to put others first, and, instead put the focus on the self.

Persistence

TEST QUESTION: *How long would you give your self to pursue your dream before giving up?*

A friend once asked me, *"Walt, how long should I give my husband to pursue his dream [of being an entrepreneur] before I insist he get a real job?"* I told my friend that a true entrepreneur doesn't think in those terms. A true entrepreneur is committed to persist <u>until</u> the dream comes true. He is committed to finding a way to make it happen. There is no time frame involved in living true to one's self. It is a life-long commitment.

Discipline and persistence combined, equate to will power. You must be able to answer the following questions positively to know if you are prepared to live true to your self:

Do I have the will power to think critically about life, about my situation, and about the world, rather than simply accept and repeat what others tell me?

Do I have the will power to "opt out" of the current system, with all its perceived perks and benefits, and to pursue a different dream and stream toward happiness?

Do I have the necessary will power to weather the storm of indifference, ridicule, opposition, attack and even the threat of annihilation, which may follow my decision to live true to my self?

Do I have the will power to risk my own present individual happiness and safety (and perhaps the happiness and safety of a group) for the sake of a future happiness and safety?

Do I have the will power to persevere even after many years, perhaps even a lifetime, of effort?

If you can answer yes to these questions, you will surely have what it takes to quit smoking, change your diet, lose weight, change professions, learn a new skill, discover your purpose, or pursue your life's passion—in other words, to live true to your self.

> **Living Truism**: In order to live true to your self, you must possess the discipline to delay, and the power to persist.

Next: Living True Test #3

The Living True Test #3

How to know if you've got the right priorities

TEST QUESTION: *What is more important to you, freedom or security?*

This is sort of a trick question. There's no right or wrong answer to it, really. I'm not suggesting that the two are mutually exclusive—that you cannot have both. People who value security can live true to the self just as much as people who value freedom. However, what I've found is that many people who are consciously aware that they are not living true to their selves report that they have, indeed, chosen security over freedom, while the majority of those who are living true do place freedom above all else. So what does your priority say about you?

> **Living Truism**: In order to live true to your self, you just might need to value freedom more than security.

~

Discipline, persistence and freedom as a priority; if you do not believe you have these qualities and focus, then close this book now and point your attention elsewhere; or, keep reading to see how you just might be able to develop those attributes and perspectives!

Living True 101 (Student Edition)

A Career Day Primer for "students" everywhere

As I sit to write a book about living true to my self, I've just been asked to speak at the annual Career Day at Marianas High School, here on the island of Saipan. The only challenge, as I see it, is that I don't really know what my career is!

By traditional definitions, I *had* a career at one time, but I gave that up to live true to my self. These days, what others would refer to as my "career" doesn't fit neatly in a box, and it isn't easily defined by a single profession, a single industry, or a single role, but by the honoring of my purpose, the pursuit of my passions, the fulfillment of my desires, and a personal commitment to live true to my self at all times.

In any event, it's now the night before Career Day, and as I've given similar presentations to students before, here's what will likely happen tomorrow when I get there.

First, I'll share my story.

"Once upon a time, there was this civil engineer who hated his career, followed his passion, started a sideline business self-publishing his own books, made enough money to quit his job, ran away to a tropical island in the Pacific, and started a tourism business so he could give tours of the island to pretty ladies every day, embark on his nomadpreneur lifestyle, and live true to his self."

Then, I'll tell them what I actually do from day to day.

At any given time, depending on the needs of the moment, the requests of my clients, or the mood I'm in, I might be writing a book, coaching other aspiring *passionpreneurs*, designing websites, composing columns, consulting other business owners on internet marketing, or selling the virtues of Saipan as a destination for tourists, expatriates, nomads, and new residents. At other times, you'll find me basking in the sun on the rocks on the northern end of the island, or cooking vegetarian meals for me and my friends.

I can do this because I don't separate my career from my lifestyle. In other words, what I choose to do every day "for a living" is determined by the lifestyle I want to live. Many people choose their jobs, professions and careers based on how much money they will make. I choose mine based on how much personal freedom and control it offers me, and by how much it allows me to find and live true to my purpose.

Someone will probably ask me what that purpose is.

My purpose, as I see it, is to teach others alternative ways of being, thinking, and acting in order to discover their own truth about their selves and why they are here.

Then, someone will probably ask me what my passion is.

Most of what I do revolves around writing and communication. The talent I have that helps me fulfill my purpose, create products to sell, generate income, and choose my "career" is my ability to string a sensible sentence or two together to communicate valuable ideas.

Through my writing, I am able to create books that I believe have value. Combined with what I've learned about Internet selling, I then create (write) websites that communicate that value, and encourage people to purchase.

Then, someone will probably ask how much money I make.

I'll artfully dodge the question, because…
- How much money *I* make has no bearing on how much you can make. (In my own consulting practice, I've often helped people make more money than I do!)
- If you follow my advice and pursue your passion, your own "career" will look nothing like mine. So that would be like deciding if you want to become a baker, by asking a candle-stick maker how much money she makes!
- In my country, it's considered rude to ask that question!

However, I will mention, as a teaser, that when I wrote my first book, and started selling it by mail-order way before the Internet came along, I made enough money to match my civil engineering income!

Then, I'll share what the bottom line is for me.

Because I live true to my self, I get to choose my clients, my business partners, what sorts of products I will sell, and what sorts of industries I will get involved in. In other words, I get to choose how I spend my time. I'm not controlled by a boss who sets my salary. I don't get stabbed in the back by co-workers who want to get ahead, and I always reserve the right to simply walk away from clients and situations I consider unsuitable. Now, being so selective about how I spend my time may or may not be the formula for becoming fabulously wealthy, but it's part of the formula for living the life of my own choosing, rather than someone else's, and that's my own bottom line.

Someone may ask what he or she should be doing now.

Your mission, starting now, and definitely before you get to college, is to determine your purpose, find out what you're good at, and look to create something of value to share with the world so that you can "create" your way to wealth and prosperity, rather than "compete" with others for it. If you simply look for a job, you'll always be in competition with others who want the same job. However, when you create something new based on your talents and passion, you earn money based on creation, not competition.

A lifestyle and wealth generated by competition can always be taken away from you if someone faster, cheaper, flashier or younger comes along. However, a lifestyle, and the ability to create wealth, based on creation are yours forever.

Then I'll suggest, "The Desire is the Power."

The *desire* to do a thing is an indication you have the *power* to do that thing. The urge you feel to play the piano, paint, draw, write a book, compose music, help others, save the environment or teach others is the universe's way of seeking full expression through you. Your desires are your innate abilities seeking to push their way out into the world. It may require training and practice for you to become better at a thing, but just the fact that you have the desire is evidence of something seeking expression.

By the same token, the lack of desire to do a thing—your lack of interest in playing the piano, drawing, writing, composing, etc.—also provides valuable information. You see, where there is no interest, there is no power. That should be honored, too, and you shouldn't force your self to do a thing you don't have the interest, desire or passion to do. That will lead to frustration, dissatisfaction and lack of fulfillment in life.

Then, I'll probably complicate the issue by saying:
At the same time, it's also important to attempt new things to discover what you're good at, and what you really enjoy. That's what your education and life are all about.

Then, I'll share the proof and the payoff!
Someone asked me recently how successful I've been at pursuing my passion. My answer is that the fact that my books exist is proof that there was something of value inside me that was seeking expression. The fact that people purchase them is proof that others recognize this value. The feedback I receive from customers who've been helped to pursue their dreams as a result of the information in my books is proof that the books are helping me fulfill my purpose. The recognition I receive, *(e.g.*CNMI Senate Resolution No. 15-54 here on Saipan)* is proof this value is acknowledged in a wider context. Finally, the fact that doing this sustains me financially and provides me with the freedom I seek—that is the ultimate payoff!

Yes, the payoff for me is that I have the freedom to choose where I want to live, and as a result, rather than living a frustrating life in a cold climate, stuck in a career that someone else chose for me, doing something I don't enjoy doing just to earn money, I have the honor and privilege of doing what I am here to do, doing what I love to do, turning my passion into profit, and living true to my self, so I can be here today on a beautiful island, on a warm, sunny day, surrounded by bright, intelligent students, eager to learn new ways of thinking and being, so they can be all that *they* want to be! What a career!

*CNMI: Commonwealth of the Northern Mariana Islands. A 14-island chain in the Pacific, of which Saipan is the capital island.

Why aren't YOU living true?

There's really only one reason

Someone once asked me, *"Walt, you've been doing workshops and consulting for some years now. What do you think stops people from starting their own business?"*

I didn't even have to think about it. I replied, "It's their belief level."

It's that simple. You might think that it is (lack of) intelligence, finances, information or some other reason that prevents people from becoming entrepreneurs. While these may be a person's *stated* reasons for his or her reluctance to start a business, the reality is a bit different.

People don't shy away from starting their own business because of their actual intelligence level, their actual level of finances, or the actual level of information and skill they possess concerning the business process. No. They fear, and talk their selves out of starting businesses because of what they <u>believe</u> about their intelligence, finances and skill. That's a subtle, but major distinction. The *belief* about a situation often has no bearing on the reality of a situation. Or, stated another way, the belief about a situation often becomes a person's reality of their situation.

The truth, however, is:

If they believe it is possible for "people like them" to succeed, they will do it, regardless of what others think.

If they believe a thing makes sense to do, they will do it, regardless of what others think.

If they believe that something can be done, they will do it, regardless of how smart, capitalized, or informed they are.

If you've ever entertained the idea of starting a business but talked your self out of it, then despite whatever reason you gave, please consider this:

If you believed that a "<u>down</u>" economy was the best time to start a business, you would act differently. *Fact: many fortunes were built during America's Great Depression.*

If you believed money was <u>not</u> a pre-requisite to starting a business, you would act differently. *According to legend, when Colonel Sanders started his first chicken restaurant, his income was a $105/month Social Security check.*

If you believed that high-school dropouts actually perform *<u>better</u>* in business, you would act differently. *Fact: director, Quentin Tarantino; automobile business mogul, Henry Ford; McDonald's founder, Ray Croc; comedian, George Carlin; news reporter, Peter Jennings, and serial entrepreneur, Richard Branson all dropped out of high school.* Of course, a good education helps in business. So, if you are already in school, I'm not encouraging you to drop out. However, if you're at an age or in a situation where going back to school might be a little challenging, then I want you to know that you can still succeed.

If you believed—I mean really believed—that "people like you" (insert your identity of choice here, e.g. women, men, short people, old people, etc.) made the best entrepreneurs, you would act differently. *Fact: Successful entrepreneurs come in all shapes, sizes and hues.*

No, really. Stop and think about that for a minute. All of the examples given above challenge what people typically believe true about starting a business. They believe an "up" economy, a lot of money, higher education or certain other traits and circumstances are necessary for business success. But how would you behave if you discovered that all the things you think are holding you back are actually the perfect set of circumstances for your success?

The same is true for anything else in life, including living true to your self on any level. Your belief level is what holds you back. It's really the only reason.

> **Living Truism**: Once a person believes she can do a thing, she is more likely to get that thing done.

A screenplay called YOU

Over the course of a weekend a few years ago, I had the exciting experience of observing a casting call and auditions for a movie that was to be filmed on the island of Guam. Would-be actors showed up by the dozens to read and vie for their hoped-for roles.

The next day, I attended a director's workshop hosted at the University of Guam, where the film's director, Alex Munoz, shared a few insights into the art of directing a movie, as well as some interesting things about how to construct a good story. For me, the most interesting part of the lecture was a simple line he shared about what makes a scene and a movie effectively "work." (More on that later.)

So, based on my introduction to the world of feature filmmaking, I'll share with you some of the elements* of a good movie/screenplay. As you read each element, I encourage you to see how these elements apply to any "drama" going on around you (presidential elections, social unrest, etc.) In particular, however, I'd like to suggest you use these same elements to create a film based on the story of your life, as if you were writing a screenplay for a movie called *The Story of Me: Living True to My Self!*

A good story always begins with a "What If?" question.

A good story starts with a "what if?" What if this happened? What if that happened? Frame your story as a single sentence identifying the hero of the story and what he/she wants to accomplish. Who is trying to stop him/her? What happens if he/she fails? Examples:

What if a group of tree-hugging environmentalists suggested the creation of a marine protected area in an effort to save the environment, but were opposed by others who saw the protected area as a threat to their interests?

*selected excerpts courtesy of www.screenwriting.info

What if a naïve, young, garment factory worker traveled thousands of miles in search of a better life, but found the conditions in the strange new country even worse than those she left back home?

What if a frustrated civil engineer decided to live true to his self, quit his job, pursue his passion, move to China, but met with challenges and opposition from all around him?

What if, you woke up one day, and realized that everything you believed about life... was a lie?

Identify your characters

The next step in telling a good story is to identify and develop your characters.

e.g. "Judy Hall is seeking a life of simplicity and love. She believes there is someone special out there seeking the same thing in her. She is determined to find it. She starts out hopeless, fearful and desperate, but by the end of the story is empowered, courageous and fulfilled."

Contained within the above description, we also have perfect examples of the four elements of a good character: (Remember, this is about *you*, not Judy Hall!)

1) NEED: What does the character want, or get or achieve?

2) POINT OF VIEW: How does this character view the world?

3) ATTITUDE: What is this character's attitude and opinion?

4) CHANGE: What is the change? Characters must change. This change is called the "arc." Every character in a good story has an arc. An arc is the change the character goes through during the story. For example, a character may start out as timid, but by the end of the story becomes courageous. A character may start out arrogant, but by the end of the story becomes humble. In order for a character to hold our interest, there must be a transformation of some sort.

Wants

A good story is moved along by knowing what each character wants. Every character wants something. According to one screenplay writing website: "There is always something at stake in a good movie. Not just something someone wants, but something that must be acquired, no matter the risk, as in the Ark of the Covenant that Indiana Jones pursues in *Raiders of the Lost Ark*. Or something highly desired by as many main characters as possible, like the hidden cash in *It's a Mad, Mad, Mad, Mad World*. Sometimes it can be an intangible thing, like the freedom of a people in *Lawrence of Arabia* or *Gandhi*. All these things drive the character's quest. It can be something personal (romance), or something that is for the good of all (saving the world from aliens), but it must be powerful and grow more desperate as the story unfolds. That something can be freedom, love, sovereignty, money, revenge, etc. What follows are seven of the most common filmmaking wants. (Which might apply to *your* story to live true to your self?)

1) Survival: Many good films are about survival, human instinct, do-or-die situations. 99 out of 100 of the top-grossing films are stories with characters in do-or-die situations.

2) Freedom, safety and security: The need to find a secure/protected setting once again.

3) Love and belonging: Someone is longing for connection or wanting to feel loved.

4) Esteem and self-respect: Wanting to be looked up to, and be recognized for their skills.

5) The need to know/understand: Curiosity, understanding how things happen and what they endure to get answers.

6) The aesthetic: Trying to be connected with something greater than themselves—a higher power.

7) Self-actualization: The characters' inner need to express themselves—to communicate who they are. The audience roots for someone to succeed. A lot of comedies have this plot.

Conflict

Conflict. This is the heart of drama. There are always obstacles to every quest. Someone wants something, but people and things keep getting in the way of them achieving the goal. At times, the obstacles can be common to both hero and villain, and the ultimate goal a laudable one for both parties, as in *Jingle All The Way*. In that film, Arnold Schwarzenegger and Sinbad battle to achieve the same goal: the acquisition of the last popular action figure for sale that Christmas season. Both have promised their sons, and they must not fail. Conflict and obstacles can be physical or emotional, but they have to be in your story, or you don't really have a story. In most stories, the main character will also have an inner obstacle, some mental or spiritual challenge, that will be resolved by the time he or she achieves the outward, physical goal of the story. (What's the conflict in living true to your self?)

Hope and Fear

Here is the line I alluded to earlier that I found interesting: *The thing that makes a scene compelling for the viewer/observer—and makes a good story "work"—is the Hope & Fear dynamic.* As you are drawn into the developing arc of the character and his or her wants and needs, you—the viewer—experience a hope and a fear in regard to the outcome of each scene and the outcome of the overall story.

For example, as you watch the story unfold, you <u>hope</u> that James Bond finds the killer, but you <u>fear</u> he will not.

Without this hope versus fear dynamic, a story does not hold your interest. Interesting, isn't it? The compelling dynamic of your own life, which has you hooked as both director and observer—and the reason you purchased this book—can be distilled into this simple statement: *"I hope I can live true to my self, but I fear I cannot."*

It's no coincidence that storytelling mirrors the human experience—that art mirrors life. What is also true is that you, as the director can guide the movie along the way you envision it. So, let's shoot some teaser scenes from this movie called "You," and create a trailer—a preview—of things to come!

A preview of things to come ▲
What will your life be like when living true to your self?

To create your preview, revisit the *Living True Test #1* and complete your answers using this guide below:

1. Have you identified your purpose in life?
ANSWER: Yes! I know why I am here, what I have come here to do and experience. I am here to _____
_____
_____
_____

2. Are you in control of how you spend your time?
ANSWER: Yes! I have obligations and commitments, but I am the one who set these as my priorities. Each day, I _____
_____
_____
_____

3. Are you actively spending your time in activities that help you fulfill your purpose?
ANSWER: Yes! I am living out my purpose by doing the following: _____
_____
_____
_____

4. Are you involved in any activities that are at odds with your ethics simply for survival or a paycheck?
ANSWER: No! I live by the following personal code of ethics that has meaning for me, and is non-negotiable and inviolable.
_____
_____
_____

5. Are you involved in any relationships that are at odds with your ethics simply for survival or a paycheck?
ANSWER: No! I live by the following personal code of ethics that has meaning for me, and is non-negotiable and inviolable:
_____
_____
_____

6. Are you living in the location and lifestyle of your happiness?
ANSWER: Yes! I wake up each day and here's what I see and do: _____
_____
_____

You get to choose

That's the whole point

The preview worksheet above, as well as Living True Test #1 upon which it is based, are based on my personal criteria for living true to my self. The point of living true to your self, is that you get to choose *your* criteria for what it means. Although I believe my criteria are universal, some of them may not be as important to you as they are to me. However, you can use them while you develop your own.

In choosing your criteria, you must be honest with your self. When you choose, ask, *"Is this the best that I can do? If I knew I could not fail, what would I wish my life to look like? Is this what I really want? Or, am I settling for something less?"*

Just because you've given up dreaming, and resigned your self to work for someone else; just because you're tired of disappointment and have given up launching yet another business idea; just because you've got mouths to feed and have given up dreaming that things could be different, does not mean you are living true. *Living true to a condition or situation you've settled for is not living true to your self.* You might be living true to, or aspiring towards a reasonable facsimile of your self, but it is not your highest self. Living true to a condition or situation that is possible to be changed, is not living true to your self. That is called settling.

Once you establish your criteria, only you will know if you are settling or not. Only you will know if you are lying to your self. Only you will know if the bar you've set for your self is where it is because you're afraid to aim higher and set loftier goals. Be honest. Then be brave. Choose the higher self.

> **Living Truism:** Living true to a condition or situation you've *settled for,* one that causes you unhappiness, and that can be improved, is not living true to your self. (Tip: all situations that cause you unhappiness can be improved.)

~

To help you choose the highest definition of what it means to live true to your self, I'd like to suggest some criteria for, well, for choosing your criteria! I suggest that to determine and define what it means to live true to your self, you must satisfy (a) a personal, yet universal definition of living, (b) a personal yet universal definition of truth and (c) a personal, yet universal definition of the self. Here are mine.

Part TWO
PRELIMINARIES

*"You cannot be happy
in a world you do not understand.
You cannot understand
what has not been defined.*

*Seeking definition, therefore,
is the first step towards happiness."*
~ Walt F.J. Goodridge

How I define living true to MY self

It's different for everyone, but....

I'm sitting on an Air China flight about to land in Beijing, People's Republic of China, where, in a few moments I'll be starting a new life adventure. Living true to my self. I just spent the last four years on the tropical island of Saipan, in the Pacific, enjoying sun, sand, sea and beautiful scenery. Living true to my self. Before that, I increased my belief level and my entrepreneurial skill set, walked away from my nine-to-five job, and escaped the rat race. Living true to my self.

What I'm doing is nothing special, really. Many people quit their jobs. Many people become entrepreneurs. Many people escape the rat race. I imagine there are others who have become nomadpreneurs. Many people escape to tropical islands because they worship sunshine. Many people travel to China. However, I think the subtle difference is that I didn't do it for the money. I didn't relocate to find or keep a job. I don't travel according to a tourist timetable or within the parameters of an "allowed vacation days" schedule. I do it all simply for the experience and the adventure. I do it for the freedom. I do it because it calls to my heart. I do it because it fulfills my personal definition of living true to my self.

What it is not

You might think living true to my self means putting my needs and desires first—that it means *me first, me only, me always, my way or the highway*. That's just selfishness. As such, it would hardly be distinguishable from a self-indulgent focus on pleasure-seeking and immediate gratification.

It's quite the contrary, in fact. Living true to my self often means living true to the *not-yet-manifested, future* concept of my self. Such a commitment requires the ability to delay gratification, and instead focus on activities and practice behaviors that will bring that future concept of me into being.

In other words, when I choose to fast this week, for instance, it's not because I wouldn't enjoy eating my favorite foods even more. It is because I am living true to creating the future, healthier me, and this requires the discipline to delay.

You might also think that living true to the self goes hand in hand with not caring what other people think. Right?

The truth is I *do* care. As someone who is committed to sharing my life for the benefit of others, I do care what others think and what they know about me. I do want them to know that I am living true to my self. I do care that they get the correct impression of who I am, and who I strive to be. I do care that I am seen as kind and compassionate among a host of other traits and attributes that are important to me.

That's the self-concept I wish to project to the outside world. What I *do not* care about, however, is *how* they judge my decision and my life. My life is what it is. I know it will inspire some, amuse others, and offend still even more.

The decisions I make are not made to stand out, or to please or annoy others. They are made to be true to my definition of my self, to what I believe is best for me and the achievement of my goals, and how I believe I need to live my life true. However, once made, I am aware those decisions do make me stand out, and that they do please some and annoy others, and that's okay. I am completely at peace with the effects of my thoughts, decisions and actions.

What it is

For me, living true means recognizing those areas in my life with which I am dissatisfied, and then doing something about that dissatisfaction, and not allowing inertia or procrastination to keep me stagnant and settling for less.

For me, living true means identifying the aspects of my life that make me happy, and giving my self more of those.

For me, living true means constantly assessing both the dissatisfaction and the elation, and using them both to evolve towards my higher self.

For example, once I recognized that living in New York and working at a job that I hated felt like a slow death, no amount of money or status could keep me there. To stay would have been to condemn my self to unhappiness. That would not be living true to my self.

Therefore, in order to live true to my self, it is necessary that my choices—everything I believe, think, say and do—achieve the following:

They must support my survival.
They must help me in discovering who I am.
They must help me grow physically, mentally & spiritually.
They must help me perform my function.
They must help me fulfill my purpose for being here.
They must help me be creative.
They must provide a certain amount of fun and joy.
They must help me offer unconditional love to my self and others.

Therefore, for me, living true to my self may be defined as:

"Making the daily choices in all areas of my life that are in the best interests of my survival, evolution and prosperity, that aid the ongoing achievement of the highest physical, mental and spiritual objectives of which I am capable, that are based on the most correct assessment of reality I have available, and that honor the evolving truth of who I am and who I choose to be, all in the personal pursuit of freedom, function, fun, as well as the highest good of all."

~

But, I'm getting ahead of my self. Let me share with you how I arrived at that definition.

Word by word
Defining living, true & self

Before I could live true to my self, I first had to decide what that actually meant. Now, at the time I made my earliest decisions in my journey, I didn't actually sit down, plan and contemplate that this is what I was doing—at least not consciously. There was no real awareness that the way I wanted to live my life was in any way going to be viewed as "living true." It's just something I did as a natural outgrowth of who I am, and what I wanted for my life.

It's only in analyzing it now, years later, that the consistent, underlying themes of my decisions have become clear. It has only now become clear as I attempt to find a logical sequence of thought and action that might be of benefit to others who want to do the same.

In any event, my point is that I cannot "live true to my self" unless and until each word in that idea has been adequately defined. In other words:

1. I cannot <u>live</u> true to my self unless I am clear what <u>living</u> is.

2. I cannot live <u>true</u> unless I know what <u>truth</u> is.

3. I cannot live true to my <u>self</u> without a clear concept of my <u>self</u>.

> So, the critical questions become:
> What is Living?
> What is True?
> What is the Self?

Living Truism: In order to live true to your self, you must seek definition and clarity.

What is LIVING?

"Doing what you want to do is life. And there is no real satisfaction in living if we are compelled to be forever doing something which we do not like and can never do what we want to do." ~ Wallace Wattles

Escape from Flatland

[Excerpt from *Turn Your Passion Into Profit*]

"Within the first fifteen minutes of my first day at my first job, I realized beyond the shadow of a doubt that I hated being there. What I saw on that day scared me to the core, and haunted me until I left seven years later. I saw mostly men, and a few women, who were living lives of quiet desperation. People who, at age 50 and above, had spent their lives allowing their dreams, and thus their spirits, to stagnate. I met men who long ago had given up dreaming about doing more, who had settled for living out their most productive years in the claustrophobic confines of cubicles, engaged in personally unfulfilling work just for the sake of a paycheck. I met others who, at my young age of twenty-one, were already planning their retirement. I met people who had bought into someone else's roles and expectations and were acting out a script without question or concern that there was something more.

They reminded me of the characters in *Flatland* by Edwin A. Abbott, a book I read in high school geometry class. The inhabitants of Flatland are flat geometric shapes living on a flat surface, who can think only in one dimension since the concept of height (a third dimension) is one that has no meaning in their flat world. I felt like that lone inhabitant of Flatland who discovers the existence of a third physical dimension. In attempting to explain what he discovered, he is met with resistance, ridicule and scorn, but most frustratingly of all, there was simply no one else he could relate to or who could understand him. He was all alone in his awareness.

As I met more and more of my co-workers at my job, I, too, felt more and more alone in my awareness, as I discovered I had less and less in common with them. They all relished the comfort of working at what veteran employees called "the country club," a worker's paradise known for its great benefits, little real stress, and which rarely, if ever, laid people off. Many felt they had truly made it, and all that was left to do was fit in, make as few waves as possible, draw a steady paycheck, earn their yearly two-percent raise, and enjoy the ride. To me, they were one-dimensional figures living in a mental flatland, unaware or unwilling to conceive of anything more.

My soul felt imprisoned, and I was determined to set it free. Unlike most of my "flatland" coworkers, I dreamed of more. I dreamed of doing something that I could really get excited about. I dreamed of a lifestyle where, instead of being locked away from the world for a third of my life during the daylight hours of every day, I had the freedom to decide when to rise, when to have lunch, when to work and when to relax. One of my fantasies was simply to have the freedom to go see movies in the middle of the day. I spent the next seven years doing everything within my power to realize that dream.

Yes, it took me several years to do it, but I finally created my own perfect "passion profit" lifestyle. I'm earning money in ways that allow me the most freedom. I create new products—using my skill for writing and talent for teaching—to share what I know so that others may grow. The products are advertised in classified ads I run in specific trade magazines, and by word of mouth, giving me the benefits of a 24-hour sales force. They are also marketed over the Internet, which is like having a 24-hour storefront operation that doesn't require my presence. Customers order my products online or by mail, and a fulfillment company ships out the orders. I can run my business from a laptop on a beach, and don't ever need to be tied down to a particular physical location. I've turned my passion into profit, making money doing what I love, helping others to do the same, and, true to my personal vision of freedom, I finally have control of my days to go see movies in the middle of the afternoon!" *[End]*

Yes, to live true to my self, I had to be willing to question what I believed was reality; challenge what I believe about my self, about others, about the world and about the universe I live in. I must be willing to walk where I believe there is no footing; act where there is no script; take risks without the assurance of success. Whether that change is a new job, a new life, or a new relationship, success requires that I see beyond the limited dimensions of my current existence, escape from Flatland, and really live!

Yes, for me, living means, first and foremost the escape from Flatland. However, there's more to living than escape.

Survival and purpose
How shall I survive? Why am I here?

It's been said there are only two questions and their answers that are of ultimate importance to every member of the human race: (1) *How shall I survive?* and (2) *Why am I here?*

"How shall I survive?" is the most basic question. Every decision a person makes in life is made in the interest of his or her survival or, more accurately, what he or she *perceives* is required for that survival.

Once a person has adequately answered that question, and secured some workable means for survival, he or she typically starts to ask more advanced questions about life and its purpose. W*hy am I here?* is the yearning for more meaning in one's life. It encourages advanced, abstract thought, liberates minds, and moves societies towards enlightenment and empowerment. In other words, individuals and societies prosper only after they stop worrying about basic survival.

Living, therefore—at the very least—in order to be meaningful, must address these fundamental concerns: to help you survive, and help you know why you are here.

However, it is impossible to truly survive, thrive and prosper, or to know and experience the reason for your existence, unless you are "free" to do so.

Freedom

It is my contention that people can best survive when they are free.* Freedom, therefore, is the most important imperative. So what is freedom?

There are only two basic freedoms of real value: a place to exist, and the time to do as you please. In other words, without a place to call your own on which you can create and cultivate the means for your survival (i.e. land), you are never truly free. And without control of your time to do the things you desire, you are never truly free. A "place to call your own" means a place that you own free and clear and that does not require payment of any kind in order for you to exist on it. You are not free if you have to pay someone for a place to exist.

The "time to do as you please" means the time to devote to any exercise or endeavor you choose without interference, obligation or contract. You are not free if someone else is in control of your time.

That is all you need in order to be free, survive, and prosper: a place to call your own, and the time to do as you please. (This supposes, of course, that at least some of that land and/or at least some of your time is devoted to creating sustenance in the form of food to eat, and shelter in the form of protection from the elements as required.)

Everything else you have been led to believe necessary for your happiness and freedom, is contrived. Cell phones, cars, refrigerators, stereos, beds and television are not necessary for survival, or happiness, peace of mind, contentment or true prosperity. Yes, they provide convenience and comfort, but ultimately, they are not necessary for happiness and prosperity.

Living, therefore—at the very least—in order to be meaningful, must include some semblance of freedom.

---

*One may argue that none of us is truly free as long as we are earthbound and existing in a world that is controlled by others with overriding agendas. However, I'm simply addressing how one can carve out a fulfilling life even within that broader context.

Function

Life is the performance of function.

I like the definition of life found in Wallace Wattles' *The Science of Getting Rich*. According to Wattles:

"You must want real life, not mere pleasure or sensual gratification. Life is the performance of function, and the individual really lives only when he performs every function — physical, mental, and spiritual — of which he is capable, without excess in any."

He elaborates:

*....the performance of every **physical** function is a part of life, and no one lives completely who denies the impulses of the body a normal and healthful expression."*

*"...the person who lives for pleasures of the **intellect** alone will only have a partial life, and will never be satisfied with his lot."*

*"... The joys of the **soul** are only a part of life, and they are no better or nobler than any other part."*

"... eat, drink, and be merry when it is time to do these things; in order that you may surround yourself with beautiful things, see distant lands, feed your mind, and develop your intellect; in order that you may love others and do kind things, and be able to play a good part in helping the world to find truth."

Living, therefore, must include the performance of function.

Fun!

And by that I mean, MY kind of fun!

I once had an interesting discussion with a friend. While we were at a party, he watched me decline treat after treat, beer, soda, French fries, and eventually turned to me and asked, "So what *do* you eat?!!"

As I shared and concluded my list of food choices, he was aghast that it didn't include the heavenly taste of chicken and pork, the euphoria of alcohol, or the compelling flavor of *MSG-laden chips and dip.

"So after all that," he joked, "heaven forbid, you step outside the door, and get hit by a truck!"

Good point, it suggests that even after all my efforts to be healthy, there are certain things I can't control. It might also imply my life of no meat, no alcohol, and no smoking is depressing, lacking, or based on some sort of enforced deprivation I would regret or change if I saw that truck fast approaching. In other words, it assumes I'm not having fun! The truth is, I enjoy a different kind of fun.

I enjoy the fun that comes from never getting sick; the fun that comes from being able to live on less hours of sleep; the fun that comes from the freedom from fear of illness; the fun that comes from having (ahem) youthful stamina and the feedback that comes with that; the fun of freedom from a pervading sense of mortal decline that says I must squeeze all my living in between ages 20 and 30, and then accept an inevitable deterioration; the incredible lightness of being and heightened creativity that comes from operating in a toxin-free body and an unclouded brain. I'm sure it seems austere to some; and perhaps, I'll never convince you my diet of coconut water, fresh local fruits, vegetables and vegan treats is as pleasurable to my palate and person as beer, pork rinds and pizza is to yours, but the fact is, it's my kind of fun!

Living, therefore—at the very least—in order to be meaningful, must be fun....however you define it!

My summary of LIVING

Therefore, my personal definition of LIVING is: *the ongoing achievement of the highest physical, mental and spiritual objectives of which I am capable in the pursuit of freedom, function and fun.*

MSG: monosodium glutamate. a known carcinogen used as flavor enhancer in many packaged foods and food preparation.

What is TRUE?

The purpose of truth is freedom.
The purpose of lies is control.

There are two very important things to know as it concerns truth. (1) The people who have the correct (i.e. truthful) assessment of reality are the most successful. (2) The only way to control someone is to lie to him.

Therefore, your mission—of utmost importance if you are to live true to your self—is simply (a) to arrive at the truest assessment of reality you can, and (b) to recognize and escape the lies that control you. That is all you need to do in order to achieve success in life, and to live true to your self.

Why living true is important

According to *A Course in Miracles*, the single greatest fear and misperception that afflicts mankind is the belief in separation—that we are alone, separate and powerless. Nothing is further from truth. Spiritualists, metaphysicians, occultists, philosophers and history's most inspired thinkers teach that on a spiritual level we are all connected; we are all one; that separateness is an illusion. In the most enlightened moments of meditation and ascension, those who have such experiences will tell of their feelings of oneness and connectedness to all things. All other fears stem from this belief in separation, and result in thoughts of insufficiency, lack and non-survival. These thoughts manifest in the following ways.

When you are not living true to the truth about money, you experience poverty.

When you are not living true to the truth about abundance, you experience scarcity and lack.

When you are not living true to the truth about the body, you experience illness.

When you are not living true to the truth about relationships, you experience desperation.

When you are not living true to the truth about food, you experience hunger (even if you eat three meals a day).

The good news is that these experiences can be remedied, reversed and removed by specific truths.

However, before we address what those specific truths might be, it may be important to understand something about the flip side of truth: lies.

The power of lies
It's about control

One of the most profound thoughts I ever heard is this: *The only way to control people is to lie to them. People cannot be controlled by the truth.*

Think about that idea in all its applications and permutations, and the depth of the concept will astound you. If someone is controlling you, it is because there is a lie in effect. Conversely, people who *feel* controlled have bought into, accepted, or are perpetuating a lie that has been sold to them.

Similarly, if you, as a person in power, wish to control the masses, you can only do so through deception. Truth, by its very nature, is freeing, liberating, and empowering. Truth frees those who offer it, and empowers those who receive it. It becomes more and more difficult to control someone the more empowered with truth they become. Leaders know this.

Similarly, a relationship built on lies is a relationship with control as its goal. A relationship where someone feels controlled is one based on lies.

If you feel trapped, powerless, helpless, or at the mercy of other individuals or outside forces, it is because you have bought into a deception—a distorted perception—of reality, of others and/or of your self. In order to live true to your self it is imperative that you recognize that deception.

How to recognize lies

The following is an excerpt from *The Ageless Adept* that defines what lies are.

"...And that hindrance, my friend, yes, the greatest obstacle to health and advancement..." the Adept began, *pausing for dramatic effect.*

I waited with baited breath.

"...is deception."

I pondered the statement for a moment. "So who is doing the deceiving?" *I asked.*

"Good question," he said, *"But before you answer it, let's explore and understand the nature of deception. This will serve you well in any discussion. So let's start by broadening our definition of what a lie is.*

"Anything that omits the truth is a lie.

"Anything that distorts the truth is a lie.

"Anything that reduces truth is a lie.

"Anything that is intended to replace truth is a lie.

"Anything that delays revelation of truth is a lie.

"Now, there are two types of lies. There are lies of commission and lies of omission; in other words, things that are done, and things that are not done; things said, and things left unsaid. There are overt and subtle acts of deception.

"There are many levels and layers to the deception blocking society's advancement. Some of it is conscious deception. Some of it is unconscious deception. Those in possession of truth consciously suppress it for their personal advancement. Then, others who are fed the lies as truths unwittingly perpetuate the beliefs, and thus become unconscious co-conspirators in the deception. [End excerpt]

Yes, it is an unfortunate fact of our society that much of the basis of what we believe to be true is actually based on deception to increase the wealth and control of a relative few. So, how does one discover what is true in an attempt to live true to one's self?

The distraction of debate
Don't get caught up

One way to discover where truth is hiding in our society is to look where so-called "debates" exist.

So, what's wrong with debate, you ask? There is inherently nothing wrong with real debate. However, despite what we've been led to believe, there are, in fact, few real debates. There is only the battle between *truth*, and *control*.

Remember, truth leads to freedom, while lies lead to control, and control is synonymous with power. Therefore, when you hear the media using the term "debate" or "controversy," it *really* means someone's power is being threatened. In a society in which truth is often subverted in the interests of advancing the agenda of those in power, debate is used to mask that real agenda.

In what passes for debate in our society, the only thing that gets decided upon in the debate is who gets the control and the power. As a result, debate in our society has become synonymous with deception and delay. It is a distraction from what is really happening. Think, for example, about the "raging" debates over smoking/non-smoking, meat-eating/vegetarianism, or the danger/safety of cell phone usage.

What is really happening is this: our society is based on lies. However, as more and more people become increasingly aware of the existence and the depth of the lies, what arises is a new agenda based on truth. This new agenda of truth challenges the lies and threatens the power of those who seek control, and that's when the so-called "debates" ensue. Without a vested interest in control, there would be no debates. It's really that simple.

If you can understand this, things will make much, much more sense.

Living Truism:
Debates + Controversy = Distraction + Misdirection

The fallacy of freedom

The reason these debates are allowed to continue unchecked; the reason the agendas they mask are allowed to continue unchallenged, at least in the minds of an unwitting public, is that people are basing their arguments and their apathy on what I call the "fallacy of freedom."

The thinking goes something like this:

"It's a free society. Everyone's point of view is valid, and everyone is entitled to believe what he or she wants to."

There is a "disconnect" here. The disconnect occurs because people interpret "freedom" to mean freedom from accountability and responsibility:

"It's a free country. I am free to smoke cigarettes and I don't need to be accountable."

In business, they interpret the "free" market to mean the freedom to kill, destroy, and exploit, without consequence:

"It's a free market, I am free to sell MSG-laden products and don't need to be accountable."

All points of view are NOT valid

So, with all due respect to the healthy and democratic exchange of ideas we've come to associate with the concept of debate in a free society, the truth is: all points of view and all agendas are *not* equal.

As an example: The truth is that smoking is unhealthy. Smoking is harmful to the smoker, to the people who breathe the "second-hand" smoke, and to the environment. The world will not make sense, and you will make poor survival decisions, if you allow others to convince you that smoking is as equal and valid a choice as *not* smoking.

As another example: The existence and state of the meat industry creates illness for those who eat meat, leads to illness for those in the vicinity of meat factories who suffer the contamination of air and water supplies, promotes suffering for sentient beings, and has a host of other dire practical as well as ethical consequences. The world will not make sense, and you will make poor survival decisions, if you allow others to convince you that producing and eating meat is as equal and valid a choice as not.

I grant you that this may simply seem like substituting one rigid dogma and agenda—theirs—with another—mine. Fair enough. The difference, however, is that the two agendas are inherently motivated by different outcomes, assumptions and fears. Judge for your self:

(1) The underlying assumption of a truth-based agenda is that we want a cleaner environment, optimal health, to safeguard freedom and human rights for our selves and others, and a correct, useful understanding of reality. (This is in contrast to entities that are polluting the environment, harming public health, violating human rights and promoting a dysfunctional understanding of reality for their own benefit.)

(2) The underlying fear of those entities—their big fear—is that the masses will adopt a new idea that will put someone out of business. If everyone believed smoking was bad, and did the next logical thing (stopped smoking), then the cigarette industry would crumble. It's really very simple.

In other words, *debate* and *controversy* are really smokescreens for known truths that threaten corporate profits. Whenever you hear of some debate on an issue with opposing sides, it is typically the side of truth that is seeking to safeguard the environment, health and/or the rights of others, versus the side of corporate profits. It's that simple.

Debate delays us getting on the same page. Debate puts us back at square one each time we engage in it, so we never move forward in a sensible way. Debate covers up what's really going on. Debate is a distraction.

The bottom line

So, why is this important? The answer is that you cannot live true to your self if someone else is distracting you with debates about your beliefs, thoughts and actions.

You cannot make effective survival decisions if what you believe about your self, about others, and about the world and universe are based on lies and are constantly being challenged by debate. In order to live true to your self, you must get beyond the debate and accept (a) there *are*, in fact, objective truths that serve an agenda that is in all our best interests as a planet, and (b) that all points of view are not valid. Some are just plain wrong and evil.

In order to live true to your self, you must arrive at a set of absolute, non-debatable set of truths on which to base, and from which to proceed with your life. If you do not, you will constantly be distracted and misdirected by each new debate lobbed at you by people with their own agendas.

From now on, whenever you encounter a debate, identify (a) the side of truth, and (b) the side of control. Choose the side of truth, and then move beyond the debate. Think critically, and ask your self: *"What is the truth? Who says so? Could there be an agenda behind this "truth?" If so, what is that agenda? If I believe and act on this version of truth, whom does it benefit? Is this really in my best interests? If I want a cleaner environment, optimal health, to safeguard freedom and human rights for my self and others, and a correct, and useful understanding of reality, what should be my truth?*

What if?

What if we could get beyond debate? What if we could really all get on the same page? What if we all agreed on certain values and moral codes? What if, once and for all, we stopped debating the obvious, and actually started to act responsibly based on what we all, deep down, know to be really true? What if we had a workable understanding of reality that helped us make sense of what is happening in the world and in our lives? And what if, instead of allowing them to engage in deception and delay, we held people in positions of power accountable to act in ways that respected these truths and this perception? Perhaps this might be the perfect "what if" to start writing the screenplay of a new way of living.

Living true in a world of lies

So, how do you find what is true in a world based on falsehoods? Uncover the lie, and then do the next logical thing.

Start with the assumption that everything you believe might be a lie. Think critically. Ask questions. Observe. Read. Experience. Meditate. Intuit. Listen. Test. Validate. Become your own authority. Make a decision, then act accordingly.

As an interesting exercise, I'd like to challenge some of societies debates and held beliefs. You'll find, as many have, that the greatest deceptions that have been perpetrated relate to our beliefs about health, illness, medicine and the body. What would your response be if I were to say to you the following?
- *Global warming exists.*
- *Vaccines are harmful and are based on faulty assumptions*
- *Sunlight is good for you.*
- *Water alone can cure many illnesses.*
- *Meat consumption is unhealthy.*
- *Milk does NOT do a body good, and is, in fact, lethal.*
- *99% of things sold in supermarkets as food are poison.*
- *Sugar is a drug.*
- *Cell phones, microwaves and x-rays are all are harmful.*
- *Capitalism, as practiced, is unsustainable.*

> **Living Truism**: In order to live true to your self, you must arrive at some absolute, non-debatable set of truths on which to base, and from which to proceed with your life. If you do not, you will constantly be distracted and misdirected by each new debate lobbed at you by people with their own agendas. Choose the side of truth, and then move beyond the debate.

If statements like the ten offered above are, in fact, true, are you prepared to delve deeper into why people are taught, and firmly believe, their complete opposites? If you are, be warned. The depth of the deception goes very deep, and there are consequences to attempting to live true to your self outside of the deceptions.

The danger of living true

"In a society ruled by lies, the truth is considered subversive. But the most beautiful thing about truth is that it grows in power the more it is shared. As more people share the same truth, the dominant lie loses power, the new truth becomes reality, and all becomes as it should be." ~ The Ageless Adept

As you compile the new set of truths to help you negotiate life and live true to your self, you would be wise to keep them to your self. At least initially. Why? Because many of these "new" beliefs challenge the norm and threaten the status quo. They are often empowering beliefs that threaten the power and control of those who currently hold it, and those who serve them. When people start to live according to a new reality, someone's power and control is inevitably threatened.

As such, depending on the level of your commitment and the nature of the threat you pose, you can expect to be ignored, challenged, ridiculed, ostracized, discredited or attacked outright. You may even have your societal freedoms and right to earn a living forcibly taken away from you. Such has been the case of doctors who have attempted to practice alternative healing based on an assessment of reality and truths that threaten other interests.

Remember what happened to heavyweight champion, boxer, Muhammad Ali when, living true to his self and new reality, he publicly and vocally refused to fight in a war for which he was being drafted? The boxing commission stripped him of his license.

This is not meant to frighten you, but simply to remind you that there are often real dangers to living true. It's the nature of the game.

My summary of TRUE

Therefore, my personal definition of TRUE is: *that which is consistent with the most correct assessment of reality I have available.*

Bonus: Once we know the truth

Once we know the truth of words that others hide behind
we won't be swayed by rhetoric, or trust as men made blind

Once we know the truth of why men do the things they do
then nothing's random anymore, for every act's a clue

Once we know the truth behind the world we see with eyes
Then form becomes a plaything that we mold as needs arise

Once we know the truth of in whose image we are made
then miracles become the norm and dreams our lives pervade

Once we know the truth of soul and know from whence we've come
we'll know our purpose and just where we'll go when day is done

Once we know the truth of time, and how things come to pass
we're freed for our eternal souls fear not what cannot last

Once we know the truth that things are perfect as they are
we never question circumstance, we simply raise the bar

Once we know the truth of things that others seek to hide
then all the news that's fit to print won't stem this rising tide

Once we know the truth that by our choices so we live
we never judge or blame, and so it's easy to forgive

And once we know as truth that love's the basis of all things
we turn our focus in to find the power that truth brings

by Walt Goodridge

This is a sample of what I call a "life rhyme." Every week, for nine years, I shared a new such rhyme-based, "living truism" with my online subscribers. For the complete archive, visit www.LifeRhymes.com or order *Life Rhymes for the Passion-Centered Life.*

What is the SELF?

Be that self which one truly is.
~ Soren Kierkegaard

The more you know about you
of soul ages, life themes, personalities, and more

It will seem quite obvious once I've said it, but you cannot live true to your self unless and until you have a clear and correct concept or picture of what that self is. Most people, however, live their entire lives without appreciating the essence of their self-hood at deeper levels, and without exploring alternative points of view of who we are as human beings, how we are constructed, where we come from, why we are here, what drives us, and what determines our natures.

I, for one, believe there is something more to me—to us—something unseen. I strive always to learn more about what that something more means for who I am. I question the boundaries of what it means to be human. I identify with my self as a spiritual being in physical form. I pursue mastery of the self. I ask different questions, and I entertain, research, test and validate other theories and paradigms that offer contrasting viewpoints to explain who we are.

Am I a body? Am I a soul? Did we evolve? Were we brought here as a species? Where do my desires come from? Why am I not like my brother? Did I, in fact, choose to be born here and now?

I believe there is untold value in the quest for these answers—value that can help me live truer to my self. In order to explain what I mean, let me tell you what I've come to know about *my* self over the years as a result of that quest.

One of the first revelations I experienced about my self occurred as part of a team during a sales training course. We all took a personality test as part of our orientation to become top sellers in a network marketing business. The results of the test categorized us as different types of fish. Some people discovered they were fun-loving "dolphins," others were money-hungry "sharks," still others were service-oriented "whales." I fell among the fact-and-figure-focused "urchins."

The point of the test was to impress upon us that the people we would be working with—as well as those we would be selling to—were motivated by different things; that no personality was "better" than another; and that all were necessary for the functioning of our team and for society.

Once I learned that my personality type was not unusual, that it was actually comprised of known, identifiable and recognizable traits, and that there were others like me, it became easier to accept who I was. Until that moment, I had known of these quirks of my personality, but felt I was alone in my uniqueness. Now, I knew I was simply a person more comfortable with facts and figures. Yes, I was an urchin!

This new awareness explained a lot. It explained why I ended up as a civil engineer. It explained why I was able to recall facts that my schoolmates couldn't. It explained why you could move me to action by providing me with information rather than by promising me "tons of fun" or "lots of money." As I became more secure in my personality, my team members knew they could come to me for facts and figures about our products and industry, and that my answers would be correct.

Years later, I took the Meyers Briggs test and found I was an "INTP" (**I**ntrovert, i**N**tuitive, **T**hinker, **P**erceiver), in contrast to its opposite type, an "ESFJ" (**E**xtrovert, **S**enser, **F**eeler, **J**udger). Again, I encountered a set of traits and preferences and aptitudes that described me perfectly, and added another dimension to my understanding of my self.

Next, by way of author and psychic, Sylvia Browne, came my introduction to the "life themes" concept. I discovered the theme I was living was "teacher." It explained a lot. It explained why I was tutoring other students from as early as second grade (I never went to first grade). It explains why I am drawn to write books that "share what I know so that others may grow."

Then, the concept of "soul age" came along, and again, provided me with validation of things about my self that added more peace to my life. According to the soul age concept, I am a *"sixth level old soul, playing the role of scholar, with a goal of Reduction, and a theme of Composition, operating in Observation mode, with a Spiritualist attitude, and an Arrogant feature."* (See Part 4 for more about soul ages.)

There have been many such insights into my understanding of self. According to my own Passion Personality Test, I am a "guru" (the four roles are Creator, Savior, Guru and Guide). In Chinese astrology, I am a "horse." In Western astrology, I am Pisces.

Each of these provided often accurate descriptions of my personality, skill set, motivations, qualities, aptitudes, preferences, tendencies, inclinations, career aspirations, world view, relationship styles, even favorite colors.

So, what does all this mean? Tests and classifications like these, exist because throughout history, people have recognized that as unique as we humans may be individually, there are certain common threads, patterns, recurring themes, and knowable categories that define us, our motivations, our preferences, our life choices, personalities and individual as well as group natures.

Call it whatever you will, but the point is: there is obviously an unexplored dimension to our being. There are explanations, and thus aspects of our understanding of our selves that exist outside the realm of popular knowledge. It means the more you know about how you may be wired, programmed, defined or constructed, the better able will be to question, re-define and embrace that programming, and recognize similar programming in other people.

(Links to all the tests mentioned are at www.waltgoodridge.com]

The case for changing the self
Just remember: Body, Beliefs and Behavior

We cannot, nor should we all want to have the same personality, skill set, motivations, qualities, aptitudes, preferences, tendencies, inclinations, career aspirations, world views, relationship styles, or favorite color as everyone else. However, certain endeavors in many areas of life *do* require that we adopt or develop certain of the same skills and qualities in order to succeed. So, the question that always arises, which underlies all personal development books, courses and philosophies, is "If who I am is based on some degree of "wiring," is it really possible for me to change?"

The answer is *yes*, and if you're reading this book, then, at the very least, you have the *hope* that this is true. Therefore, if you ever find your self in a debate—internal or otherwise—over whether people can change, then simply remember the three Basics of Change: Body, Beliefs and Behavior.

Your <u>body</u> changes. Any physical attribute you have now that you did not have when you were six months old is the result of change.

Your <u>beliefs</u> change. Any belief you now hold about your self, the world, and the people in it (think religion, politics) that you didn't have when you were six years, old is the result of change. All learning is change.

Your <u>behavior</u> changes. Any habits you have now that you did not have when you were sixteen years old are the result of change. All habits are learned. All learning is change.

In fact, everything in the known universe exists within a paradigm of constant change. Nothing ever stays the same. Things are either expanding or contracting, increasing or decreasing, improving or deteriorating. Absolutely nothing is the same at this moment as it was just ten seconds ago.

What this means is it *is* possible to change. In fact, it is inevitable. This should no longer be a point of debate for you.

> **Living Truism:** In order to live true to your self, you must arrive at a more expanded concept of your self from which to proceed with your life.

At the same time, as a result of some of this wiring, there is, in fact, a sort of "limit" to how much we can change, and therein lies the fatal flaw of many personal development philosophies, books and courses. Let me explain.

The fatal flaw
Why most personal development courses fail

"...try as I might, it's just not that important to me!"

Let me use my own discovery of my soul age as an example. When I first read the description of a classic "old soul" it was like looking in a mirror. Much of what I had privately known and believed about my self, my interests, motivations, and feelings, were staring back at me—documented and known! It was like coming home.

Suddenly, a lot more of what I had always thought was a mystery, now made perfect sense. Suddenly, things that I had only secretly suspected about my self found validation. In some areas of my life, I stopped struggling. In other areas, I renewed the struggle with more conviction. I finally felt like I "fit in" somewhere. I now knew why some things were infinitely important to me, while other things were just not that important at all. (A similar thing happened when I read *Bringers of the Dawn*, by Barbara Marciniak.)

Now, the concepts that resonate with you will likely be different. You may not be an old soul, you may not be a "light bringer," you may not be a teacher, a guru or a horse, etc., but can you now see why some personal development courses are doomed to fail? They may work for many people who are living out a "young soul" existence, for instance, but won't do a thing for the old souls or the infant souls. They may work for one person whose life theme is "catalyst," but may not work for one whose life theme is "artisan." (Even *this* book, written by a known old soul, might only reach other old souls who can relate to me!) And it won't be because these souls lack motivation. It won't be because they don't work hard enough. It won't be because they are defective in any way. It may simply be that the truth of that person's self may rest in the realization: *"try as I might, it's just not that important to me!"*

Your mission is to find—within the truth about your self—what *IS* that important. This brings us to a key concept in the quest for change.

Change becomes you

*"Change occurs when one becomes what he IS...
not when he tries to become what he is not."*
-- Arnold Beisser, Gestalt therapist

According to Arnold Beisser (who was referring to effecting change in systems, organizations, and societies), change *"requires that the system become conscious of alienated fragments within and without so it can bring them into the main functional activities by processes similar to identification in the individual."* He goes on to say, *"Disparate, unintegrated, warring elements present a major threat to society, just as they do to the individual. The compartmentalization of old people, young people, rich people, poor people, academic people, service people, etc., each separated from the others by generational, geographical, or social gaps, is a threat to the survival of mankind."*

"We must find ways of relating these compartmentalized fragments to one another as levels of a participating, integrated system of systems."

Again, Beisser was referring to systems, organizations, and societies, but the concept is applicable (as he indicated) to individuals. The "warring elements" and "compartmentalized fragments" within each of us include our often-fragmented identities, the dichotomy of our competing work life/home life roles, our public/business persona versus who we really are or wish to be. The truth, as Beisser indicates, lies in finding the truth within us, and becoming that entity that is a uniting of the often competing elements of our identity. In other words, you must live true to the self that you are within. You change through becoming who and what you already are within.

Choosing reinvention

Reinvention, therefore, is an act of becoming.

Of morals and ethics

As you might imagine, the topics of morals and ethics is an important one in creating a valid concept of living true to the self. So, let us gain some clarity there as well.

Morals are what a <u>society</u> decides are in its best survival interests. This varies from society to society, and what's frowned upon by one society can be perfectly morally acceptable in another.

A moral code, therefore, is a series of agreements developed over time that guarantee the survival of a specific group—the group, in this case, being society.

Morality is a group thing.

Ethics, on the other hand, is the study of the general nature of morals and of the specific moral choices to be made by the <u>individual</u> in his relationship with others. It's based on one's personal beliefs about what is right and wrong.

An ethical code, therefore, is the set of certain restrictions indulged in to better the manner of conduct of one's life. A person conducts her self according to such a code because she wants to, or because she feels she is proud enough or decent enough or civilized enough to so conduct her self.

Ethics is a personal thing.

Choosing my ethical code

I won't always agree...

    I'd like to share a little story about a man who was once challenged to defend his life choices. The following is a brief excerpt of a public speech he gave in explanation.

    "Ladies and gentlemen. So that you will all understand me and my choices, let me tell you a story.

    "A few years ago, I met a young lady who became my girlfriend. She would visit my house on occasion and, at the time, as I was living in a tropical island, there would be the occasional fly, mosquito, lizard, or brigade of ants roaming through my apartment.

    "The first time this happened while she visited me, my girlfriend, upon seeing the ants in my apartment, started to make moves to kill them. She asked me if I had some bug spray. I told her no. I also asked her not to kill them. "Just let them be," I requested. She thought I was crazy. When I have a fly in my apartment, I open the door or window and guide it outside. When lizards appear, I catch them and toss them out into the front yard. The reason I don't kill those living things, my friends, even though it's not against the law, and presumably no court would fault me for killing ants, is because I've decided that it is inconsistent with my philosophy of life. I make my own decisions as to what my philosophy will be, regardless of what is "allowed" by society,

    "Similarly, the reason I don't kill *people*, my friends, is not because it's against the law. It's because it is also inconsistent with my chosen philosophy.

    "As a free human being, I reserve the right to choose my philosophy and act according to it.

    "There's nothing wrong with deciding what is right and wrong. That's what societies do. When a society decides what is right and what is wrong, it's called a moral code. A moral code is any behavior that the society deems necessary for its overall survival. Typically, everyone agrees to the moral code and the society survives. Those who do not agree, are typically ostracized, punished, incarcerated or otherwise forcibly separated from the masses.

"Now, I'm not naive, nor am I a rebel for rebelliousness' sake. I understand that societies survive best when people agree to and adhere to these moral codes. I also understand that, ostensibly, laws are put in place to safeguard the rights, safety and survival of others. So, while I might like to drive 90 miles an hour on the streets, I choose not to, because doing so puts me and others at risk. Setting the speed limit at 40 mph in our small town is a law that makes sense. Therefore, I follow the law because it makes sense to do so, not because police officers will give me a ticket.

"Therefore, while I may not always do what the masses do, there are many things that the masses do, that I willingly participate in. I drive on the right side of the road, just like the masses do, because I recognize it's silly and unsafe not to. However, I don't eat meat, despite what the masses do, because I recognize it's silly and unsafe to do so.

"So, having said all that, my friends, I befriend whom I wish because I choose to do so. I give to whom I wish because I have the unalienable right to do so. I live the lifestyle I do because I can. I share my lifestyle and knowledge with those who request. I make no apologies, I ask no permission, and I have no guilt or remorse over doing so, regardless of how you choose to judge my lifestyle, or stigmatize those whom I befriend, give to, or share with.

"My actions are not dictated by a fear of the consequences of externally imposed philosophies, laws or authority, or the judgment of you or other men. I do what makes sense given my ideals and worldview. I do what aids the survival of the whole according to how I see things. I do what makes me happy without infringing on the rights and freedoms of others while doing so.

"The philosophy I live by, therefore, is a simple one. I've decided that my beliefs and actions will be guided by the following ideals:

"I do what is consistent with natural law as much as is practical.

"I honor the law of cause and effect.

"I strive to honor the rights and freedoms of others in all that I do.

"I assist others whenever and wherever possible as long as their own ideals are consistent with my ethical code and do not require that I compromise my own.

"Some people choose what is accepted. Some people choose what is easy. Some people choose what is expedient. Some people choose what is profitable. Some people choose what they can get away with. Some people choose only what is within parents,' preachers,' politicians' or the power structure's prescribed lines of behavior. Some people choose only from the options given to them and those endorsed by the society at large, because they feel they have no choice but to agree. I choose what suits me, my friends, because…I don't always agree."

> **Living Truism:** In order to live true to your self, it is necessary to establish your own ethical code, mindful, but independent of the group mentality.

~

As you've no doubt surmised, I am the man in that story. There are things I believe, choices that I make, and behaviors I engage in that stem from my own ethical code regardless of what is considered morally acceptable by the wider society. I apply that code and strive to live true to my self in all areas of my life.

In all areas of my life

In order to really live true to my self and my ethical code, it is not enough to have—or profess to have—a particular philosophy or set of beliefs. Living is "thinking, speaking, choosing and acting...." Therefore, to really live true to my self, I must *act* from those beliefs. I must put that code—those beliefs—into practice. I must apply the same criteria to, and live true in, all areas of my life.

I live true to my self when it comes to... **Freedom**

Before graduating from Columbia University with my Bachelor of Science in Civil Engineering, I was offered two full-time positions. One was from Con-Edison, the utility company, for a $30,104/year salary. The other was from the Port Authority of NY/NJ at $29,276/year. "Con-Ed" wanted me to start the week after graduation. The "PA," however, said I could start whenever I wished. I chose the PA's lower salary as I wanted to take the summer off to start a venture a friend and I were contemplating. Things didn't work out as we had hoped, but the point is, for me, it's always about the freedom.

I live true to my self when it comes to... **My purpose**

I've since come to know that I am a teacher. Everything I do is about imparting knowledge, information, inspiration, ideas, experience and guidance to others. Even in the enjoyment of blogging about my nomadpreneur travels, I seek to share insights and observations that fulfill that purpose.

I live true to my self when it comes to... **My lifestyle**

At this point in my life, I define my self as a minimalist, vegan nomad. *"I function with less, won't eat any flesh, and my home's where I rest."*

I live true to my self when it comes to... **How I make money**

I never liked working as an employee. I enjoy my freedom, and I want to honor my purpose and turn my passion into profit. Therefore, I have constructed a method of income that is entrepreneurial, internet-based, and does not require my presence at any fixed location; a method of income that helps me teach others, and that provides an outlet for my passion for writing and communicating; a way of making money that provides a passive, residual income stream. *No slavery.*

I live true to my self when it comes to... **Where I live**

I don't like cold weather. I am happiest and feel most alive when I can sit in hot, burning, "oppressive" sunshine and sweat. Therefore, I choose to live on a tropical island or similar latitudes. *No compromise.*

I live true to my self when it comes to... **My image**

Many years ago, I was offered many thousands of dollars to do a *Turn Your Passion into Profit* workshop at an event at a major venue in the states. I turned it down. The event was being sponsored by a cigarette company. I just couldn't see my self standing on stage with a big cigarette ad on a banner behind me. Even though I would be delivering information on self-empowerment and business success, I would be associated with, and indirectly supporting, the improved brand-identity, and agenda of the sponsoring company.

On another occasion, I won a trip for two to a tropical island. Part of the requirement and terms of accepting the prize was that my name and/or photo could be used in future promotions for the company. The sponsor was an alcohol company. I refused the prize for the same reasons. Everything matters. *No sell out.*

I live true to my self when it comes to... **My time**

People may steal my money. People may steal my ideas. People may steal my possessions. However, I can make more money; I can come up with new ideas; and 99% of the objects I possess can be replaced. However, my time is irreplaceable, the most valuable asset I have and thus the thing I'm most vigilant about how it's spent. I don't spend time or expend energy on people or situations that are a waste of either. *No distractions.*

I live true to my self when it comes to... **My health**

I am vegan. I eat no meat (and for the record, fish are not vegetables), no dairy or eggs. I don't smoke or drink alcohol. I eat one meal per day, primarily a raw food diet, and I sublimate my sexual energy. I don't believe my body was designed to thrive on canned, processed, pesticide-sprayed, nutritionally devoid, preservative-laden, heat-pasteurized, artificially-flavored and colored, unnecessarily cooked, irradiated food. I believe my body is adversely affected by cigarette smoke, car exhaust, industrial fumes, air conditioning; that my skin is harmed by chemicals in soap, carcinogens in shampoo, dyes in make-up, formaldehyde in plastics. As my own authority, I have proven my health is better, energy level is higher, perception is clearer, my creativity heightened, and my stamina enhanced when I live true to these beliefs.

I've been vegan since 1992, and while I always leave room for new ideas, this is generally not a subject open for debate in my life. I will not compromise, not even *"just this once, Walt?"* for special occasions, cultural sensitivity, to be one of the guys, or because it looks good. *Nothing artificial.*

I live true to my self when it comes to... **Relationships**

It's obvious to me that the cause of relationship unhappiness is that people make promises that are inconsistent with their true selves, their wiring or their will. As a result, their partners form certain expectations. When the promiser's actions catch up to the promises, and are found inconsistent, mayhem ensues. It's so much simpler, albeit not easy, not to have to look over your shoulder, hide or lie in a relationship. In my own life, I tell my partners what they can expect of me, and offer them the opportunity to stay or leave. For when the actions catch up to the promises, there will be consistency.

The communication, in essence, proceeds like this:

This is who I am. This is what you can expect of me because I live true to my self. This is what I expect of any lover. These are my preferences. These are the things I like. These are my non-negotiables. I will not mislead you. I'm not going to lie and promise you something I have no desire or intention of providing. I hope you will operate at that same level of truth and disclosure. Now, therefore, given our individual expectations, wants and desires, are we, in fact, compatible? Would you like to be my girlfriend and play in my sandbox?

Of course, there are trade-offs. When you live true, the available pool of potential partners may shrink since most everyone else is playing according to society's norm. But, just imagine how much less deceit, distress and perhaps even divorce there would be if more people simply had the courage to live—and love—true to their selves. *No skullduggery.*

I live true to my self when it comes to... **Spirituality**

An acquaintance once asked me about my religion.

Him: So, Walt, what's your religion?
Me: That's a leading question.
Him: I mean, are you a Christian?
Me: [I paused to find the right answer.]
Him: Well, are you Muslim?
Me: Those aren't the only options, you know. The question is not as bad as the ever-popular *'Have you stopped beating your wife?'* trap, but it's like asking, 'what kind of gun do you carry?' It starts with an underlying assumption that doesn't step back far enough to a place of non-judgment and objectivity.
Him: Ok, well do you believe in God?

Me: Again, the question is flawed. Forced to answer, I would say yes, but that really doesn't tell you anything about me. For one thing, you don't know whether we actually share the same *concept* of God. My god could be a turnip, for all you know.

What's important, for me, when I meet or do business with someone is not what particular religion she claims to belong to, but to see if she shares the same sense of personal ethics and a moral compass that makes us compatible. Many crimes against humanity have been committed in the name of religion. Many Klansmen claim to be good Christians, and many terrorists claim to be good Muslims.

What matters to me is a person's overall belief system and whether their actions are consistent with those beliefs.

The point is, I've noticed that many people don't use even their own religions to guide their ethics and behavior. Simply observe how many people engage in business practices that exploit the disadvantaged, compromise their values for a pay check, drink, smoke, curse, abuse their bodies, kill animals for sport, (and condemn others for doing all of the above) while professing to be followers of a particular religious doctrine of peace, brotherly love, temperance and forgiveness.

They use religion as a "Get out of Hell Free" card to absolve their selves of the destructive, malicious behavior they willfully engage in while here on earth. *No controlled show.*

I live true to my self when it comes to... **Business ethics**

Recently, some friends and I had a discussion about different products upon which to base a business. Their view was that a business owner merely fulfills a need for the public.

Them: If the public wants meat, sell 'em meat. If they want MSG, sell 'em MSG. If they want cigarettes, sell 'em those too. One product is just as worthy as another.

Me: But what if I believe smoking cigarettes is personally, publicly and environmentally harmful? And, what if I don't believe people should kill and eat animals?

Them: People have a choice. You're not forcing them to buy it.

Me: True, but even though I'm not the one doing the killing or smoking, wouldn't I be violating my own personal ethics by selling something that contributes to the killing of animals or that negatively affects people's (as well as my own) health? Just so you know where I stand: if for some reason I had a can of soda lying around my house, I <u>wouldn't</u> offer it to a guest to drink, since I believe it's poison, even if *they* think it's food.

In many cultures and mindsets, there seems to be an underlying belief that business is merely about filling a need; and that a "good" business to get into—meaning a business that can make "big money"—is usually and necessarily ones that pander to vices, or not-so-healthy desires.

To determine where you stand on this, you might ask:
- *As a business owner, do I simply provide a need, and simply sell whatever is "legal" to sell regardless of my own beliefs?*
- *Should I personally sell a product I know to be harmful?*
- *Or do I offer the world something that moves it in a positive and uplifting direction--according to my own beliefs?*
- *How far will I go in the furtherance of my business agenda?*
- *How do my personal code of ethics & moral compass guide me?*
- *What does my belief system—my religion, as it were—tell me is right and wrong for me to do?*, and, a question I ask my self
- *As a coach, do I help others succeed in business if they choose to sell products that are not in synch with my own beliefs?* (Do you know my answer?)

In business, my own choices are guided not by how much money there is to make, but whether I feel good about what I am selling. *No flim-flam.*

I live true to my self even when it comes to... **Blogging!**

Remember that quote I used to open this book? (*"Success in any endeavor depends on the degree to which it is an expression of your true self."*) Well, I received validation and confirmation of the truth of that quote from, of all places, my blogging. Almost immediately upon beginning to write about my "Jamaican in China" adventures, several people wrote to me saying the same thing almost word for word: "Walt, I never knew you had such a great sense of humor!"

Now, this wasn't my first experience with blogging. After several false starts and fizzles, I had been having difficulty maintaining a consistent frequency of posts for my business blog, and was even challenged sustaining my own excitement for what I was blogging about. However, when I started to write about the things that truly mattered to me, and write from my unique worldview as a vegan, Jamaican, minimalist, nomadpreneur, author, indulging my predilection for things Chinese, that's when things clicked! I had finally found my "blog voice" by being true to my self.

Readers who knew my business persona from years of reading my business columns, my books, life rhymes and articles, commented on the hidden sense of humor and the satisfaction that my new writing style was offering them.

Furthermore, based on the feedback, I realized the very goal with which I had started the original business blog—to inspire others to follow their own dreams—was now being more fully realized! Reading about me following my dreams and defining my self in non-traditional ways, was as much (perhaps more) of an inspiration than any cost/benefit business-style post I could ever have done! *No pretense.*

> **Living Truism:** In order to live true to your self, it is necessary to apply your chosen code of ethics consistently, without contradiction, in all areas of your life.

My summary of SELF

Therefore, my personal definition of SELF is: *the evolving truth of my parentage, programming, predispositions, presence and purpose on earth.*

Living true in the service of other selves

What about the other people?

Upon reading an early draft of this book, a friend challenged two ideas in my worldview.

What about the collective?

"It seems as if you are dismissing the importance of individuation <u>while</u> staying connected to the collective. What would be the value of individuating [i.e. living true to yourself] if you cannot share your wealth of discoveries with others?"

I'll say this about that: How often have you heard some advice prefaced by the statement: "There are only two types of people..."? Well, I suggest that there *really are* only two types of people: those who are here for the service of self, and those who are here for the service of others. The path between these ideals is a gradient. There are no *absolutely* selfish individuals, and no *absolutely* selfless individuals. Everyone falls somewhere in-between, striving towards one ideal or the other.

I believe that the orientation towards service to others is the nobler path—one that holds the key to personal growth, enlightenment and the overall good of the planet. Many of us will find our purposes in life, our greatest fulfillment, and even our greatest material prosperity inextricably linked to providing some benefit for the good of mankind. It is a paradox of nature that (a) living true to one's self and (b) choosing a life lived in the service of other selves, are often one and the same. So, no, I am not dismissing the importance of staying connected to the collective.

However, I also know that what is seen as selfish and dismissive in one context, may have an entirely different interpretation in another. Let me explain.

Having spent my formative years in the Caribbean, having received the balance of my formal education in the United States, and now by living true to my self in Asia, I've had the opportunity to compare and contrast different cultural beliefs, worldviews and customs. What is considered normal in the US—doing what you love and what makes *you* happy—has a tinge of selfishness by Chinese standards. In China, what is best for the collective—the family, the community—carries more weight than one's individual aspirations. Therefore, what I teach in the US—to follow one's passion—is never qualified with "if your parents approve," while in China, it might have to be. Remember, morality is a group thing.

What about the children?

The next issue had to do with my statement *"...even if there are children involved"* in the Living True Test. To answer the next logical question, "No I do not have children." I can only speak from my perspective as a *child* of divorce.

I am not advocating shirking one's responsibility, or abandoning one's commitment, or compromising the welfare of an innocent, or causing the internalization of the reasons for a divorce that young children often experience. At the same time, I don't believe one should remain trapped by decisions made in earlier stages of development and awareness.

It is my belief that a parent is a better parent when he or she is happy and living true to the self. It sets a better example of "the appropriate level of self-advocacy," and shows the child a healthy response to an abusive or loveless relationship. I believe leaving such a relationship serves the best interests of everyone concerned.

Of course, your programming (soul age, personality type, etc.), cultural upbringing and chosen ethical code will determine what wins as a priority in your own life. My views on these issues are simply that, and are not intended to have you change your ethical code. They're based on the best assessment of reality I have available. Ultimately, you must decide for your self where *my* self ends and *your* self begins.

Putting it all together
living + true + self =

So, here's what we have so far:

My personal definition of LIVING: *the ongoing achievement of the highest physical, mental and spiritual objectives of which I am capable in the pursuit of freedom, function and fun.*

My personal definition of TRUE: *that which is consistent with the most correct assessment of reality I have available.*

My personal definition of SELF: *the evolving truth of my parentage, programming, predispositions, presence and purpose on earth.*

Putting them all together with a few tweaks:

> **What Living True to My Self means to me**
> "Making the daily choices in all areas of my life that are in the best interests of my survival, evolution and prosperity, that aid the ongoing achievement of the highest physical, mental and spiritual objectives of which I am capable, that are based on the most correct assessment of reality I have available, and that honor the evolving truth of who I am and who I choose to be, all in the personal pursuit of freedom, function, fun, as well as the highest good of all."—Walt Goodridge

~

Living from my chosen ethical code; creating an independent lifestyle; freedom from a nine-to-five job; living where I want to live; selling products that uplift; honoring my purpose to teach; pursuing my passion for writing; spending time with the people I wish to; living a vegan lifestyle; these are a few of my favorite things.

"Yes, Walt, so where does 'happiness' fit into all of this?"

Solving for happiness

"Happiness is not the absence of problems but the ability to deal with them." ~ unknown

The whole point of living true to one's self is, indeed, to find happiness, not just purpose. Even though my definition includes "fun" as a requirement, creating enduring, long-term happiness may be something different. So, let's explore it.

A Mathematical Proof

A friend and reader of my weekly newspaper column once ran into me at the post office and asked me if I had any suggestions of techniques, philosophies, or anything I could suggest to help her "be happier."

I was flattered she asked (I guess I must *look* happy, or maybe I look so *unhappy,* that she figured I must be searching, too!) In any event, in my never-ending quest to provide value to others, I promised to email her something, and then set about figuring out what I could offer to help.

As I sat thinking about it, it occurred to me that there must be a formula—a mathematical approach to happiness, if you will—that anyone could benefit from. So, using my memories of math class, I decided to apply the concept of "proofs" to the concept of happiness!

Solving for "X"

Perhaps you recall the concept of "proofs" from geometry class? To complete a mathematical proof, we start with a "problem" or "given," and must prove a conclusion.

Given: Triangle ABC

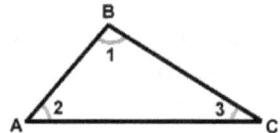

Prove: The angles of triangle ABC, (angles 1, 2 and 3) add up to 180 degrees.

In proceeding with a proof like this, you typically start with an assumption, then make statements invoking known geometric laws, principles and postulates, to arrive at the specific conclusion all in a logical sequence.

Now, I won't bore you with the actual mathematical proof for the "given" above, but we can apply the same strategy to *solving for happiness*. Let's start with a "given" and what we wish to prove.

Given: I am unhappy

Prove: That I can be happy (and if so, how?).

PART 1. What is the cause of unhappiness?

ASSUMPTIONS: 1. Unhappiness has causes. 2. Therefore, it is possible to identify, eliminate these causes, and be happy.

ARGUMENT: If you are not happy, it is because there is a flaw in your belief system.

ARGUMENT: Your belief system is comprised of your thoughts. Therefore, if unhappiness is caused by a belief system, and if a belief system is merely a set of thoughts, then:

CONCLUSION: Unhappiness, and therefore, happiness are caused by your thoughts.

[You may rightly ask, "What about my words and actions?" Yes, thoughts, words & deeds are the important trilogy we often talk about. However, since our words and our actions are functions of our thoughts, we can deal first with the thoughts, and the words and actions will—with the necessary discipline—follow suit.]

PART 2: *What thoughts must I change in order to be happy?*
ASSUMPTIONS: It is possible to identify and change the thoughts that are making you unhappy.

ARGUMENT: There are only four types of thoughts that you have: You think about your self, about others, about the world/universe, and about life's situations.

CONCLUSION: Therefore, your thoughts about: (a) your self, (2) others, (3) the world and (4) life's situations, must be changed in order for you to be happy.

PART 3: *What thoughts about my self are important?*
ASSUMPTION: The thoughts about your self cover many facets of your being.

ARGUMENT: When it comes to your self, there are three components we speak most of: body, mind and soul.

ARGUMENT: Also, when it comes to your happiness, there are three states of existence that we speak most of: Being (who you are), Doing (what you do), and Having (what you have)

CONCLUSION: Therefore, your happiness in relation to your self will be a function of, and determined by, your thoughts (i.e. your belief system) about your body, mind and soul, and about who you are, what you do, and what you have.

Suggestions for the solution

Solving for Self
The first, most important step to take to solve for happiness is to solve for the self. I suggest to you that the more you learn (i.e. solve) about your self, and change the thoughts and belief system about your self, the happier you will become.

Solving for Others
The more I've discovered about my self, the more accepting I've become of who I am, and by extension, the more tolerant I've become of other people's uniqueness (and thus

happier). I no longer expect "dolphins" to be more like "urchins," "ESFJs" to be more like "INTPs," "healers" to be more like "teachers," or "young souls" to be more like "old souls." We all have our uniqueness, our purposes, our missions, our themes, our traits, our talents, and predispositions that make us each different and vital individual parts of the whole.

Solving for Life's Situations

Another source of unhappiness for many people are the situations that arise in their lives.

Many years ago, I took a course called LifeSpring™, that introduced me to the concept of personal accountability. The most meaningful lessons I learned about life's situations involved (1) the law of cause and effect—that every effect has a cause, (2) the law of attraction—that we attract situations into our lives by our thoughts and expectations, and, therefore (3) the importance of being accountable for the situations that happen in life.

"Given that this is happening in my life, what did I do to create and/or attract it, and, more importantly, what am I going to do about it now?" Many people waste time playing the blame game, and instead of responding in ways that create their desired reality, they waste time assigning blame to people or circumstances as the cause for creating the effects in their lives. Sadly, many people never move beyond that level of response to life.

> **Living Truism:** In order to live true to your self, and be happy, it is necessary to accept accountability for your life.

~

Unhappiness with the self; unhappiness with others; unhappiness with life's situations; these all bring me to what is perhaps the most insightful statement I ever encountered in my own quest to solve for happiness:

Unhappiness is an unmet expectation

The key to happiness.
The only reason you are ever unhappy about anything, is because you have an expectation that is not in alignment with reality. Husband forget your anniversary? You're unhappy because you expected him to remember. Change your expectation. Noisy neighbors? You're unhappy because you expect everyone to value peace and quiet the way you do. Change your expectation.

Anytime you cling to an expectation that is not in alignment with the reality or truth of a person or situation, <u>you create your own unhappiness</u>, and therefore, you have the ability to create the opposite state by choosing a new reaction. That is the key to happiness. Plain and simple.

Now, I'm not saying you don't have a *right* to be disappointed when certain things happen. What I am saying is that you are able to <u>make a choice</u> of how to respond. You could actually *choose* to be tolerant when others don't behave the way you'd like them to. You could actually *choose* to smile, when the noisy neighbors act up. Choosing your responses by changing your attachment to your expectations is, in fact, the only way to create your happiness, for it is the only control you have in life. Let me repeat:

> **Living Truism:** The only thing you have complete control over in life is how you respond to the people and situations over which you have no control.

Applying the key

So, in which areas of your life are you unhappy? When asked that question, many people point to their relationships, weight, family situation, career, and any number of areas. Let's apply our new key to happiness to a few real-life situations. Of course, the challenges here are several.

First of all, many of us are so immersed in our realities, truths and paradigms, that we cannot step outside of them far enough to question them or see them objectively.

Second, even if we identify and are willing to let go of a flawed "truth," we lack *new* information from the outside with which to compare and contrast it. The process of finding new beliefs to replace old ones can be a challenging one. If it were easy, many more of us would reclaim our happiness.

Applying the key to happiness to… # Relationships

"I can't find the right relationship!"

This is one of the most common areas of unhappiness. Most of us want to connect with another for companionship, love, romance, and sex. However, our beliefs often keep us from attracting the people with whom we'd like to connect, or whom would make the best connection.

Applying the key: *Something I believe to be true, and thus my expectation about [RELATIONSHIPS, MEN, WOMEN, LOVE, MY SELF, etc.] is not in alignment with reality and truth. What might those flawed beliefs be?*

Perhaps you believe relationships deprive you of freedom. Perhaps you believe love is about control, ownership or dependency. Maybe you are suspicious of men/women. Maybe your self-esteem is such that others sense your neediness and are turned off. Maybe you're simply looking in the wrong places for the wrong things. Any number of these beliefs and expectations could sabotage your search for love.

For many years, I went to nightclubs to meet women, and for many years I never met anyone. In all the years my friends and I club-hopped—where the majority of patrons smoked and drank—I never, ever, ever met and dated anyone. (Did I mention "ever?") It turns out that all the women I *have* dated, I met in health-food stores, business seminars, or through friends. In order to remedy my unhappiness, I simply had to understand my self more (who I was, what was important to me, etc.), and change my expectation about finding compatibility in the otherwise incompatible club scene.

Applying the key to happiness to... **Health & Body**

"I do all the right things, but I still get sick!"

Perhaps your unhappiness has a physical focus, or is centered on your thoughts about your body. Maybe you think you're too fat, or too slim. Maybe you simply want to feel healthier. Maybe there is even a chemical imbalance that is causing your depression.

Applying the key: *Something I believe to be true, and thus my expectation about [*MY BODY, MY HEALTH, SICKNESS, CURE, BEAUTY*] is not in alignment with reality and truth. What might those flawed, out-of-alignment, untrue beliefs be?*

Well, you might believe, for instance, that your body was designed to digest and thrive on canned, processed, pesticide-sprayed, nutritionally devoid, preservative-laden, heat-pasteurized, artificially-flavored, FDC-colored, irradiated food, or that your body is not affected by cigarette smoke, car exhaust, industrial fumes, or air conditioning, or that your skin is not affected by the chemicals in your soap, carcinogens in your shampoo, dyes in your make-up, or formaldehyde in plastics, etc. I suggest to you that these beliefs are not in alignment with reality and truth. I suggest that all the "right" things you believe and upon which you based your actions and expectations, are not really right at all. As a result, your body is aging prematurely, not functioning optimally, and not doing the things or looking the way you'd like it to.

REMEDY: You might be surprised how much lighter, more alive and, by extension, how much happier you might feel after a week-long juice fast or water fast in which you purge your body of all the toxins you have ingested and accumulated over the years; or how a detoxifying sauna regimen and the avoidance of chemical soaps and lotions on your skin might actually rejuvenate you and ease your feelings of unhappiness; or, how simply eating more raw, fresh fruits and vegetables and less processed foods might boost your energy, trim the fat and purge your system.

Applying the key to happiness to... **People's behavior**

"Why do people do the things they do?"

Applying the key: *Something I believe to be true, and thus my expectation about* [OTHER PEOPLE, STRANGERS, NEIGHBORS, FAMILY, FRIENDS, CO-WORKERS] *is not in alignment with reality and truth. What might those be?*

Perhaps you believe that people should act a certain way, and when they don't, it makes you unhappy. Perhaps you believe that people feel the same obligations you do. Perhaps you believe people are motivated by the same things you are, and thus should share the same set of behaviors.

SOLUTION: Change your beliefs about people, and you will be happier. You have no control over what people will think, say or do. The only thing you can control is how you respond to the things people think, say or do. *Walt's Law of Obligation* says: "There ain't none!" In other words, despite what you may believe, people (that includes, friends, lovers, spouses, children, family and strangers) are *not* obligated to do anything simply because you expect them to.

Applying the key to happiness in... **Soul matters**

"What's it all about????"

When people start contemplating the meaning of life, the reason for their existence, and their identity as spiritual beings with a purpose and an afterlife (i.e. *Why am I here?*), many of those people harbor a secret unhappiness with the religious teachings to which they have subscribed in search of answers.

Applying the key: *perhaps something I believe to be true about* [THE SOUL, SPIRIT], *and thus my expectation, is not in alignment with reality and truth.*

SOLUTION: Change your beliefs about your soul to something that answers the questions you have. Earlier, I touched on the topic of soul age. When I chanced upon the concept some time ago, and discovered that I might be an "old soul," and what that meant, it immediately echoed and resonated with things I felt to be true all my life, but for which I had never previously encountered any external validation.

As I got to "know" or more accurately, become re-acquainted with the old soul in me, many questions were answered. It explained many of the seemingly unexplainable things about my self, my experiences, about others, about the world and universe we live in.

As one example, having an understanding of the soul, its existence before and after this earthly manifestation, explained why I never cried when my dear grandmother passed on. It was not because of some machismo-driven persona, but because I intuitively recognized our special spiritual connection as ongoing despite the loss of the physical one. I discovered that this response was a quite typical old soul detachment that others may misunderstand, but which has always been a hallmark of my personality and approach to life.

Applying the key to happiness in... **Politics**
It's the president's fault!

The reason many people are unhappy is because the world they live in does not make sense, and you cannot be happy in a world you don't understand. Let me be clear: you can be *brainwashed*, you can be *entertained*, you can be *distracted*, you can be *drugged*, and you can be *lulled* into a false sense of security....but you can't really be happy.

True happiness, in the world as we know it, requires people to really change. However, people resist change because change requires a new understanding in a world that already doesn't make sense. People resist change and the necessity of operating outside of a comfort zone, because, for many, it took a long time to construct an understanding of reality that seems to work—that is, one that seems to explain *"who I am, my role in the world, what others are like, and what the likely outcomes are going to be."*

For example, the reason many white people in the United States are unhappy with the election of President Barak Obama has to do with this. Despite obfuscations of the issue having to do with his identity as Democrat or Republican, Socialist or Capitalist, Christian or Muslim, citizen or not, it's clear to those who are honest, that the rejection of the US president has more to do with race. Quite simply, many whites are unhappy about having a black president.

So, let's apply the key: *Something I believe to be true, and thus my expectation about* [AMERICA, WHITES, BLACKS, MY SELF, POWER] *is not in alignment with reality and truth. So, what could those beliefs be?*

America is a nation built on the concept of white supremacy. Therefore, this is the understanding of the world many people live(d) in. If not happy, it at least made them comfortable in their beliefs. Imagine their confusion on election night, when the reality they witnessed did not match their beliefs and expectations. For them, the world (at least America) had become a place they no longer understood. You cannot be happy in a world you don't understand.

Applying the key is only half the formula for solving for happiness. In order to effectively use the key to change any of your current beliefs, you must have alternate beliefs with which to compare and contrast them in order to determine which is the most truthful and real. To be more blunt, you must have a belief system that is "correct."

My summary of applying the key

Anyone who is unhappy is operating with an outdated, ineffective belief system. The goal, therefore, is to find, create or update your belief system so it more correctly explains and defines who you are, the world and your role in it, the others who share the world with you, and accurately identifies the causes and predicts the effects of your and other people's actions. *My* belief system says that if you can find such a belief system, then happiness is possible.

The stark truth about happiness is that you cannot be happy in a world to which you are applying an incorrect belief system. You cannot be happy if everything you believe....is a lie. We'll explore this in detail in Part Four.

> **Living Truism:** You *can* be happy if you understand how to apply the key to happiness in all areas of your life.

~

In the *Living True Test #3*, I offered some questions to determine if you are indeed ready, and possess the necessary will power required to live true to your self. The reason answering these questions is important, is because there are, in fact, challenges you are likely to face on your journey, and I would be remiss if I didn't prepare you for some of them.

Part THREE
PROS & CONS

Pros and Cons: from the Latin phrase "pro et contra" (for and against)

Great spirits have always encountered violent opposition from mediocre minds. The mediocre mind is incapable of understanding the man who refuses to bow blindly to conventional prejudices and chooses instead to express his opinions courageously and honestly.
~ Albert Einstein

"Be true to yourself despite being misunderstood. It is painful but not fatal." ~ I Ching

The Pros

On practically every page of this book I've offered what is essentially my personal list of "pros" for living true to my self. However, I'll state for the record what I believe to be the greatest "pro" in favor of a life lived true, and that is that when you decide to live true to your self, you will become—both by choice, and by default—an agent of change, and an agent of truth (they are one and the same). The more in alignment you become with truth, the more you assist and inspire, both by action and by example, the path of truth and change upon which the world is bound.

As you grow in your commitment to change through truth, truth becomes your ally, and all the miracles, magic and mystery that go along with truth are activated for your benefit, and become yours to use on your own behalf and for others.

I can tell you from personal experience that my reward —achieving the freedom that drives me—as well as the resulting independence, validation of purpose, satisfaction, fulfillment, and all the synchronicities and magic I experience on a daily basis, is the greatest gift I have given to my self. Living true to my self is its own reward.

The Cons

However, every person's reward will be unique. You developed your own list of benefits and rewards in the *Preview of Things to Come* exercise. Every good thing that you imagine that life can be, is within your power to create. However, like any good thing, there are often unintended consequences, both good and bad. Here's a question that is adapted from Paul Scheele's Abundance for Life course so that you're not blindsided by the unexpected: *What do you suppose you'll like least about your decision to live true to your self?*

It's a very powerful question—the answer to which, understandably, may be beyond the realm of your imaginings, right now. However, knowing that there may be elements of living true to your self that cause a bit of dissatisfaction is an awareness that will keep you grounded in reality, and prepared for the unexpected as you proceed.

It's been said that you can have anything you want in life if you do two things: (1) get clear on the thing that you want, and (2) decide or determine the price you will have to pay in order to achieve it.

In my own experience, I've discovered that as a price for living true to my self, that the available pool of peers and partners is less. I've discovered that there is some sacrifice of fun (by some definitions) that I must forego in the early stages of creating a life lived true to my self. As a practical example, I've discovered that there are less restaurants at which I can comfortably dine, given my belief system and choices. Thankfully, none of these is fatal.

And while I cannot prepare you for all the consequences of your private experience, I *can* share with you some I've personally experienced, as well as some that all great achievers experience at some point in their journeys.

Inertia

You may experience...

People want change, or so they say. If you speak to most people, you'll discover what they *really* want is for things to change *for the better*. They want to get richer, happier, and more secure, but don't wish to get poorer, unhappy or lose a degree of security or peace of mind. However, in order to change, we must adopt new ways of thinking and behaving. Once this change takes place in our thinking and acting, by extension our experience on the planet changes.

The challenge on an individual level is inertia—the tendency of an object at rest to remain at rest; the tendency of an object in motion to remain in motion. By the time you are intellectually capable of understanding the very words and concepts that change requires, you've already had to accept their polar opposites in order to survive, and by extension, you perpetuate the very reality you need to change.

By the time you're frustrated enough with working for someone else, and making them wealthy, you're locked into a system of debt, responsibility, image maintenance, impression, shame and obligation from which it seems impossible to extricate your self.

By the time you make enough money in this system to be able to change it, you're too vested in keeping it the way it is so you can survive.

By the time you gain the courage and insight to take charge of your health, you've been trained to believe that others hold the key to that health. You've been converted to a religion of sorts that requires, and often gets, your blind faith in treatments that actually make you sicker.

In other words: by the time you're old enough and wise enough to question the belief system, you've been indoctrinated into the belief system to such a degree that opposition seems futile or contrary to your survival. By the time you're really ready to have the new life you want, you're too busy living the old life you *don't* want, and escape seems nearly impossible. If you are in motion, you tend to stay in motion. If you are at rest, you tend to want to stay at rest.

That's why change—real change—often comes when life, limb or some aspect of one's identity or survival is threatened with imminent extermination. Choices become clearer. Actions take on the necessary sense of urgency.

That's why things often must get very bad—at the brink of revolution, or at the precipice of annihilation—before they start to get good. The reality of impending doom or destruction must take hold in the mind, before people find the necessary motivation to do what must be done.

The good news is that change is essentially a challenge of will. It doesn't take any more money, any higher position or any more power and status than you currently have. You can start where you are and move toward where you want to be.

But, you may find, to your amazement, that you have within you the seeds of true greatness, the ability to lead others by the example you set, the gift of inspiring others to embrace the challenge, the talent for moving them to take the necessary actions in the interest of change. You may find, that you are indeed an agent of change—better, true, meaningful change—the world has been waiting for! You can overcome inertia.

You may experience... ## The load test

As a former civil engineer, and now as the owner of several websites, I'd like to introduce you to a concept called "load testing." In civil engineering, a structure like a bridge, or a building is subjected to weight to determine if it can and will support the loads for which it is being designed (cars, people etc.). A similar process is used in website design. Before a website "goes live" (i.e. is launched), it is subjected to a test that simulates millions of simultaneous visitors to see if it can handle (without crashing) the load of a million "hits" (visits) that a successful marketing campaign might generate.

Well, something similar happens in life, too. The moment you decide *you* want to "go live," or construct another level of success, the universe sends a load test your way. You'll know when you're being load-tested because you'll feel the pressure of everyday life increasing, or you'll find that everything you attempt seems to go wrong, or you might meet upon a hundred roadblocks that test your patience, commitment, strength and will power. You'll feel like you too are receiving a thousand hits a day, or a thousand pounds per square inch of pressure!

The question is, *Are you ready to "go live?" Can your structure support the load and the pressure?* Once it's determined that you've got what it takes, then just as in construction, another story will be added to your rise. Like a website, you'll be ready to go "live!" So, the next time you're going through an obvious load test, you can smile, because *now* you know what's really going on!

You may experience... ## The final exam

Similar to the load test are what I call Final Exams. These are typically administered by the universe before graduating/promoting you to a new level of success. Just as in academic advancement, before I can move to the second grade, I am given first grade tests to see if I learned all the necessary lessons. My responses determine if I may advance, or if I need some remedial training! Because I know I may be tested prior to each graduation, I don't interpret these exams as setbacks or obstructions on my journey to live true to my self. I see them as necessary determinants of my willingness to endure the typically more advanced, more demanding—but more rewarding—course requirements for the new grade.

If you can't handle first grade tests, there's no way you're ready to move up to second grade!

You may experience... ## The weeding

There's always a sorting or weeding-out process in effect in life. As unpleasant as it may be to accept, after all the chaos and turmoil of a situation has subsided, there will be some who make it through, and some who will not. Whether it's an economic downturn, a bursting bubble, layoffs, or natural disasters, your belief level may need some alteration in order to function in the new paradigm. This weeding out of the old may occur at any moment in your journey to live true to your self, so be vigilant, and be prepared.

You may experience... ## The reconstruction crisis

Considering pursuing your passion? Interested in launching your own business? Setting a challenging life goal? Want to live true to your self? Congratulations, and best of success to you! If what you are considering is something that will take you to places others are afraid to journey, then there is going to be a price to pay for acting on ideas that go against the norm. In addition to the ridicule and rejection you may face from friends and family, there will also be some cosmic forces at play that may seem to be working against you. However, here's an analogy to explain what may be happening.

If you are living in a house and wish to build a bigger better house, it may be necessary to demolish the existing structure to its very foundation before you start building anew. In much the same way, once this creative universe we live in gets its orders from you that you want to change your reality, forces are set in motion that begin making the necessary changes in your life. If you've been living with people who think negatively, who are going nowhere in their lives, you may find that you argue more frequently. You may realize that a person you thought you knew, has grown in an entirely different direction from where *you* are now. You may have to make some hard decisions about who to keep with you on your journey, and who to leave along the way. If not, these individuals may hold you back from reaching your dreams.

Similarly, if you've found your self in a nowhere job, and you wish for the fulfillment and freedom of living true to your self, don't be surprised if things start happening which lead to a (forced or voluntary) separation from your present place of employment.

These strange occurrences, which at first may appear to be the onset of chaos in your life, are part of a phenomenon I call "reality reconstruction." It usually happens right after a new reality is wished for and committed to significantly.

I witnessed this phenomenon firsthand in one of my business ventures several years ago. Within a few days of signing someone into my network marketing business, some "catastrophe" would invariably befall him or her. It might have been an illness, a fight with a spouse, a car accident, or some seemingly random event. At first I thought I was jinxed, or worse, that I was the one jinxing my new business partners. I soon came to realize, however, exactly what was going on: their realities were being reconstructed.

We live in a receptive and constructive universe that responds to our thoughts. When you say you want a better life, visualize it, affirm it, and set goals accordingly, things naturally start to happen to bring you the life you desire. What happens, however, is that most people miss the clues, and interpret the ensuing chaos, tension, stress, turmoil, strained relationships, disagreements, disappointments, betrayals and lack of support from those they love, as an indication they've made a bad decision. Or worse, they fail to see the connection the new way of thinking is having on relationships and environment, and get distracted putting out these seemingly unexpected, and unrelated fires in their lives rather than letting go of those relationships and environments.

Interestingly, "reality reconstruction" doesn't affect everyone to the same degree. Some people meet their dreams at a point in life after they've already gone through the necessary preparation and personal growth. For those people, it can be a smoother transition into their dreams. However, among those who are affected by reality reconstruction, many fall by the wayside, overwhelmed by the unexpected changes in their lives. Others, however, see it and embrace it for what it is: a reality reconstruction in progress.

The reality reconstruction that ensues by following a passion or living true to one's self can mean ups and downs, uncertainty of regular income, having to make late payments, having your lights turned off, having your telephone disconnected, and maybe even experiencing homelessness. I recall the months where I was basically homeless and living on my friend's couch and running my business from his living room. Deep down, I knew that this was a temporary reality that I needed to experience in order to get to the success on the other side. Nothing motivates like desperation. And for some of us, experiencing dire straits is the only way we'll ever develop the inner strength to really do what's necessary to succeed. Are you prepared for any of the possible reconstructive realities that you may experience while you build your life anew?

Some people tell me they could never go through the kinds of experiences I did. What's more, if they happen to be married with children, they add that being single would make such changes easier. In response, I encourage people not to let their *reason* for doing a thing be their *excuse* for not doing it. In other words, many people desire the living true lifestyle so they can spend more time with their children, but use the "responsibility" of providing for those children as the reason for not taking the risk to succeed.

I know of one woman with three children and a husband who quit her high-paying job to pursue her passion of being a writer. She ended up homeless and on public assistance (kids, husband and all) just before her big break—a six-figure publishing contract—came along. She didn't let the downs get her down. She knew that sunshine follows rain; that there's always the seed of victory within every defeat; that sometimes it's necessary to hit bottom, before you can bounce back up; and that all things "come to pass;" that is, they have come so that they may pass... (*if* you learn the lessons they offer.)

So, as you move forward to living true to your self, remember that change often comes with a few challenges of reconstruction. If you are prepared for these, you will have a better attitude, more realistic expectations, and consequently a better chance of achieving the goals you've set for your self!

Natural drag

You may experience...

Just like the Reconstruction Crisis, there are other basic laws of the universe that apply to every thing and every one. One such law says, *"For each and every action there is an equal and opposite reaction."* Let me give you a practical example.

Recently, air traffic across Europe's air space was grounded due to the danger of flying jet-engine planes through the airborne ash from the eruption of a volcano called Eyjafjallajokull in Iceland.

In one interview, an aviation expert was asked why the planes couldn't simply fly above, below, or around the clouds of ash. He explained that flying a jet plane below the level where the cloud of ash had been detected (8,000-10,000 feet) was not an option since the "drag" (the air resistance) on the body of the plane would be so tremendous at that low altitude as to make fuel efficiency and air travel impractical. Jet planes fly best in the thinner atmosphere of higher altitudes. [If you're interested, other reasons include that the ash was practically undetectable by the naked eye to fly around, and flying above the invisible cloud of ash would require the equally risky option of ascending and descending through it.]

What a great metaphor! So, let's fly with it!

As you go through the process of living true to your self, the resistance you may encounter may take many forms. It may appear that people are jealous. It may appear that people are sabotaging your progress and success. Some will promise and not deliver. Others may deliver, but drag their heels in doing so. It may often seem like an intricately interwoven, conspiracy designed to keep you down and push you back!

On those occasions, it may help to remember that such resistance is actually a natural part of the process, or, more accurately, part of a natural process.

Just like a jet plane attempting to fly to its destination, your forward motion toward your goal of creating a life lived true, is going to be resisted by those whose sole purpose, it seems, is to provide the "drag" of lower atmosphere. The thoughts, expectations, habits and behavior that exist in the lower atmosphere are not vindictively aimed at you; they are simply part of what exists at lower altitudes. Those who exist there can't help it. It's natural law.

The lower your aspirations, thoughts and behavior, or the people you associate with, the "closer to the ground" you will be flying, and thus, the more drag, resistance, and pushback you will encounter.

Fortunately, *unlike* the rigid, easily-clogged parts of a jetliner engine, *you* need not be grounded by such resistance. To get transcend the invisible, but destructive ash that often permeates the atmosphere of your life (i.e. your own thoughts and the expectations of others), you can simply choose to think, speak and act on a higher plane (pun intended). In other words, fly above the drags (and the fjords)!

Think big. Fly high. The atmosphere above the clouds is better for speedy and fulfilling travel...and the view is much better, too!

You may experience... **The lure of the easier game**

In a recent coaching session, a client and I discussed the "expensive" outcomes of some of the business risks she had taken over the years. I comforted her (only partly, I'm sure) by reminding her that, years ago, she chose to play a different game than the average individual. Consequently, whatever outcomes she experienced ("good" and "bad"), were naturally, and by necessity, going to be different than those of the average person who chooses to play an "easier" game.

Society encourages us to play the easier game. The easier game is called "Employee for Life" or "Live True to Someone Else's Plan for Your Self." If you opt for the security of a regular job, you can pay the bills that will keep the utilities on, keep the roof over your head, pay the car note, maintain your credit and keep everything working great! And, by the criteria of that easier game, you're high in the rankings if you manage to keep your life in relative equilibrium.

However, the game of "Succeed on My Own Terms" also known as "Live True to My Self" is naturally a harder game for the simple reasons that (1) fewer people play it, (2) the strategies and rules aren't as well known, and (3) the risks (but thus the rewards, too) are greater. Few utility companies, landlords, banks and creditors will be supportive of your choices while you work out the kinks in your strategy for playing the "harder game." So, if you choose to play it, be prepared for greater tests of your commitment, patience, perseverance, creativity, resolve, faith, endurance and stamina.

At least initially, during the early stages of constructing a life lived true to your self, it may appear—and it is in fact, true—that you will have to work twice as hard.

Remember, everyone else will be playing the easier game—swimming with the tide while you swim against it. Most everyone else will be responding to life from a reduced set of perceived options, a vastly different ethical code, and smaller screenplay roles with limited scripts.

You will have to work during odd hours, when everyone else is asleep. Sometimes it may seem as if you have to think for two (or more people). You will have to be the one to think critically, plan for contingencies, develop alternate strategies, and work *within* the system even while you work to escape it. This is par for the course. It's the nature of the game.

A different scorecard

So, if you've opted for the harder game of living true to your self (which, fortunately, *does* get easier with time), don't be misled by the apparent high scores (possessed car, clean credit, working telephone) your friends are enjoying. Remember, you chose a different game. You'll have to learn to score your self based on other criteria (freedom, purpose, fulfillment, creative expression) while you work out the kinks! Rest assured, however, the rewards make it all worthwhile!

Sticks and stones

You may experience...

I have been called
- extreme,
- obsessive,
- eccentric,
- driven
- stubborn, and
- fanatic

Those are all just words (typically with negative connotations) used to describe people who don't quite fit into the sheep mentality. They are judgments made by people who have chosen not to make waves.

At the same time, I've also been called
- courageous

- inspiring
- intriguing,
- amazing,
- unique, and
- a role model,

What some call obsessive, others call committed. What some call eccentric, others say is unique. You get the idea.

As the children's rhyme goes, "sticks and stones may break my bones, but words will never hurt me." Don't let such terms distract you. Perhaps, just perhaps, extreme, obsessive, eccentric, driven, stubborn fanaticism (or being perceived as such) is what is required to live true to your self. The payoff is you get to live your life on *your own* terms.

You may encounter... **Vested interests**

You don't need permission or agreement to choose and act on your beliefs. You are your own authority. If you seek such permission or agreement, a debate will inevitably ensue. People will argue to talk you out of your beliefs. There are usually two types of people who argue against a new belief: those who have a vested interest in keeping things they way they are (for power and control), and those who have been convinced of the old beliefs by those in the first group.

If, for example, you choose to believe you attract the circumstances in your life, and seek agreement or permission from others, you will encounter opposition from two groups: (1) those who benefit from keeping you a passive player in the visible game, and (2) those who have been convinced by the people in group 1, and will cite scientific research as well as biblical chapter and verse in support of the randomness of life, and your passivity and futility of attempting to change your reality in any significant way.

If, for example, you choose to give up eating meat and choose to eat only real food, and, for some reason also feel the need to seek agreement or permission from others, you will encounter opposition from (1) those who sell meat for a living, and (2) those who have been convinced by those in group 1 that meat consumption is healthy, and who don't want to face the possibility that their own belief system is flawed and so, cite scientific research, as well as biblical chapter and verse in support of their belief.

The vested interests and their minions will always argue in opposition to truth.

> **Living Truism**: To live true to your self, you must be prepared to weather the forces of indifference, destruction & reconstruction, resistance, opposition, attack and even sabotage in pursuit of your dream.

~

The preceding phenomena are just some of the challenges you may face in your quest to live true to your self. Next, I'd like to share a few additional challenges, as well as some suggested coping strategies, by invoking another "movie mirroring life" analogy to address what is likely the most common goal of those who seek to live true to self: the escape from the rat race!

Bonus: The Tao of Shawshank

12 Rules for Escaping the Rat Race

[This special "members-only, movie scene, director's cut version" of The Tao of Shawshank, features the corresponding film scene or theme for each of the 12 rules. It was formerly available only to my online subscribers. Please note that it contains points covered elsewhere in this book]

Tao is a Chinese word which, loosely translated, means "way." The letter "t" is an approximation of a Chinese sound with no exact English equivalent. The most accurate rendition would be a combination "t" & "d" sound, as in "Tdhow." Many pronounce it "Dow", as in "Dow Jones" (to rhyme with "how" or "now"). I give you, therefore, The Way of Shawshank

One of my all-time favorite movies is *The Shawshank Redemption* which stars Tim Robbins and Morgan Freeman. Robbins plays Andy Dufresne (pronounced doo-FRANE), a man wrongfully imprisoned. Freeman plays "Red," a fellow inmate who becomes Andy's friend and confidante.

While others cite the themes of *"transformation"* as well as *"maintaining integrity in places and situations where integrity is lacking"* as the movie's primary messages, its immediate appeal to me was what I recognized and related to as the themes of escape and freedom—concepts that figure prominently in my own world view.

With no intention to trivialize the stark reality and profound experience that one goes through when one is actually physically incarcerated, I submit to you that many of life's situations can be likened to being confined, restricted, caged or otherwise imprisoned.

When I was employed in the corporate world, I felt as if I was in a sort of prison, as if a part of me was dying each day I showed up for work. I felt trapped. Confined. Caged.

I also hate to give away the plot of a movie out of respect of those who have not yet seen it, but *The Shawshank Redemption* is a perfect metaphor for life. The movie offers a blueprint for what 90% of us in the world should know, should do, and should become in order to survive, thrive, prosper, and be free. Watch it (again) so you can fully appreciate the Way of Shawshank and the following lessons one can glean when applied to a career, relationship, etc. in which one feels trapped, stuck or otherwise restricted:

1. Sometimes life and its circumstances can be like a prison.

2. Even the innocent can be imprisoned. [*SCENE: At the beginning of the movie, despite his innocence, Andy is imprisoned based on circumstantial evidence.*]

3. Knowing the truth about who you really are (your guilt or innocence), or about the world around you, is sometimes not enough to set you free. Sometimes justice comes only to those who help their selves. [*SCENE: Later in the movie, he is kept at Shawshank by an uncaring warden, despite the discovery of new evidence that might have proven his innocence.*]

4. Some will attack you. Some will discredit you. Some will screw you over. You may have to put up with a lot of that on a regular basis. Do not let it change you. Bide your time, and build your castles in your sleep. Endure. [*SCENE: Shortly after arriving in prison, Andy is attacked and raped by "The Sisters" a gang of "bull queers" who terrorize and almost break Andy's spirit. This continues for two years until a stroke of fortune (for Andy, at least) ends it.*]

5. Plan your escape. Keep it a secret while you work on it, for even your good friends may dissuade you from having and acting on your hopes and dreams. [*SCENE: We learn later that Andy has been methodically and diligently orchestrating his escape for 10 years. At one point, his friend Red, who has been denied release for twenty years, tells Andy that hope is a dangerous thing.*]

6. Sometimes it is necessary to construct a fantasy or a facade that others see, to hide your true intentions. But just behind it, on the other side of your fantasy, behind the passion that others see, often lies your path to escape. [*SCENE: Andy requests a poster of the latest sex symbol of the day. Behind the huge poster that adorns his cell wall lies an escape tunnel he's been constructing.*]

7. One of the best ways to maintain your sanity while trapped is to find what you're good at (a passion) and do it, even if it benefits those who are your jailers, but never, ever lose sight of your ultimate goal. Sometimes it's necessary to work within and support a flawed or evil system in the process of masterminding your eventual escape from it. [*SCENE: Andy's talent for accounting/tax law allows him to earn a modicum of freedom and good favor from the prison officials and guards by providing tax consulting, trust/investment and filing services for the guards and warden. Later, he provides bookkeeping services for the warden to launder illicitly obtained funds the warden is receiving.*]

8. Feel free to break the rules of confinement on occasion, as long as you're aware of, and prepared to suffer the consequences. Do not live in fear of punishment or retaliation. They can't take your music away from you. [*SCENE: Andy locks himself in the warden's office and plays an opera record over the prison public address system. He does it to offer himself and his fellow inmates a brief but welcomed bit of humanity and beauty in their drab, duhumanizing existence. He is punished with two weeks of solitary confinement in "the hole." Upon his release, reunited with his fellow prisoners, he comments, "Easiest time I ever did!"*]

9. Sometimes, it may be necessary to accept that some people have been in prison for so long that they neither can nor want to function outside of its walls. Not everyone is seeking escape. Do not let this fact change *you*, or have you resign in your determination to be free. Use it to empower your self to walk a different path.

"These walls are funny. First you hate em'... then you get used to em'... after a while you start to depend on them. That's what it means to be institutionalized."--Morgan Freeman as "Red" [*SCENE: Brooks, a fellow inmate who spent 50 years in prison before being released, is reluctant to be set free and, after failing to make the adjustment to life on the outside, ends up taking his life.*]

10. When the time is right, execute your escape. Take action. In executing your escape, you may have to go through even more dirt, filth, and "crap" to get to the other side. Bring a bar of soap. [*SCENE: In the movie's climactic escape scene, Andy has to crawl through 500 yards (the length of 5 football fields) through a sewer pipe with human waste to finally emerge on the outside of Shawshank Prison and to freedom!*]

11. Once on the other side, you can live the life you've always envisioned, and live true to your self. [*SCENE: Once free, true to the vision of the dream life he held on to while in prison, Andy escapes to a Mexican coastal town to restore old boats!*]

12. If you want to double the fun, bring a friend and confidante along. [*See the movie!*]

The plot of *The Shawshank Redemption* mirrors an effective three-part strategy for escaping the rat race (and also the subtitle of this book): 1. Reclaim your power. 2. Break Free. 3. Live True to Your Self.

How do you reclaim your power?

In order to reclaim your power, you must first know the truth that there is, in fact, power to be reclaimed. This power is the nature of your being. You were born with it. However, for most of us, it is being suppressed.

What power am I referring to? I'm speaking of the power to create—the power to envision a specific reality and then to make that reality come true. That power can be applied to your career, your social life, your financial situation, and overall prosperity. You have the power to envision something other than what you are currently experiencing, and then to take steps to move towards that vision. A new, more rewarding career? More money? Fulfilling relationship? A different lifestyle? Purpose? Passion? Profit? It's all within your power. If you do not believe this, then someone has lied to you.

It's said that knowledge is power. In order to fully reclaim your power, therefore, you must discover what you are being deceived about in all areas of your life. As each layer of deception is exposed, your power increases.

How do you break free?

In order to break free, you must take action. Once you know that there is another way to be, another reality "on the outside," you can then break free from the cage you are now living in. You must take "risks."

However, armed with the awareness of the power you have reclaimed, you will no longer see these actions as the risks they once appeared to be. They will seem the only course of action that makes any sense.

How do you live true to your self?

The answer to that question will be different for each person. Everyone seeks a unique payoff; everyone seeks a unique experience of living, a unique experience of truth, and a unique experience of the self.

However, if you are not currently living the life you wish to live, then I suggest that you must first (re)define living. Then, as indicated above, (re)define truth. Then (re)define the self if you are to gain clarity about what life means to you.

Remember, also, that these steps are non-linear. They are not executed sequentially but as parallel processes. You will always be reclaiming more and more of your power, you will always be breaking free in different ways every day, and on many levels you will always be improving your definition of what it means to live true to your self.

One Day I'll Fly away

"I have to remind myself that some birds aren't meant to be caged. Their feathers are just too bright. And when they fly away, the part of you that knows it was a sin to lock them up does rejoice. But still, the place you live in is that much more drab and empty that they're gone."

Those words from the movie, echo what Morgan Freeman's character, Red, felt in his heart towards his friend, Andy. Your decision to empower, escape and live true to your self may remove you from the day-to-day reality of those whom you may have to leave behind. However, perhaps too, like Andy Dufresne, your escape will offer a path that others may follow to find their own happiness! You owe it to your self—and to them—to lead the way. See you on the outside!

###

[end Tao of Shawshank]

My summary of the pros & cons

Given the society we live in, living true to one's self is inherently a statement of action, risk, momentum, creation, evolution, growth, creation, flight, and work and is an action that challenges the status quo. As such, by the law of nature that requires an equal and opposite reaction to every action, your decision and progress may be met with apathy, inertia, reconstruction, weeding, resistance, opposition, and even attack by other forces. Be prepared.

~

Now that you know what you might be in for, it's time to explore a vital prerequisite for successfully reclaiming your power, breaking free and living true to your self. You need a better belief system.

Part FOUR
Prerequisite

"There will be no proof. There will be no justification. There will be no committees. There will be no boards. There will be no federal departments. There will be no "scientific" research. There will be no debate. There will be only that which issues forth logically from a sound initial assumption. You are your own authority."
~ Walt F.J. Goodridge

Why you need a better belief system

A belief system is comprised of your beliefs about the physical, mental and spiritual components of life, and what you believe about your self, others, the world you live in, the reason for your existence, and why you are here. The process of maturing is (or should be) about developing an increasingly truthful and effective belief system.

The purpose of having a belief system—any belief system, for that matter—is to help you navigate and negotiate effectively through life. The correlation between having the correct belief system and happiness and success in life is really simple: People with a valid belief system, one that is in synch with reality, make better decisions. Life is simpler, provided you have the "correct" belief system. However, without the correct assessment of reality, the world will not make sense, and you will make poor survival decisions.

Sadly, not all belief systems are created equal. Some belief systems are empowering, some belief systems are limiting. Some are just so utterly out of synch and out of touch with reality that they lead to utter disappointment and failure.

So, how do you determine which kind of belief system you currently have? You can tell how much in alignment with reality your belief system is by (among other things) how fulfilled you are, how healthy you are, and your level of peace of mind. If any of these areas is lacking in your life, it means that something you believe is out of synch with truth.

Conversely, if your life is exactly the way you wish it to be—if you are already happily living true to your self—then perhaps there's no need to entertain a new belief system. However, if you dream of living a different sort of life, then perhaps it's time to begin the search for a more accurate and effective set of beliefs about your self, the world you live in, the people you share it with, the universe as a whole, and the reason for everything. Here are some of the benefits of having such a more accurate belief system:

With a better belief system…. **You focus on the right things**

Let me give you a true example. Many, many years ago, I had a friend who, after years of observation, came to the conclusion that success and happiness in life was correlated to hair length. And, to hear her tell it, she seemed to make a good case that the girls who "married well," the actresses who won Oscars, the businesswomen who excelled, all had long hair, while the girls with short hair fared poorly. She was convinced of this, and it was part of her belief system. While aspects of it may in fact be valid, I hope we can agree that such a belief system is essentially flawed.

Sure, you may argue that getting her hair to what she perceives to be the right length may indeed make her more self-confident, which in turn may make her more successful but, by and large, having this belief system—which is out of synch with reality—has her focus on developing the wrong attributes, limits her belief in her potential (if she has short hair), and has her expecting that if she gets long hair, that everything will magically change, that people will treat her differently, and she will be happy and successful.

The world is full of people with many beliefs like this that determine how they *act (e.g. dishonesty is necessary for wealth, short people cannot be as successful as tall people, the illegal aliens are to blame, illness is random and unpredictable, the FDA is looking out for my best interests, etc.)* At some point, however, people's beliefs come face to face with the truth and reality of a situation and those beliefs will either pass the test or fail. You will only get so far based on the length of your hair.

People with the "wrong" belief system focus on the wrong issues, are limited to certain degrees of freedom and potential, and expect things to unfold in a certain way. If their belief systems are not based on reality, then their focus will be misguided, their potential will be limited, and their expectations won't be met—which, as we know, is the single cause of unhappiness in life.

With a better belief system.... **You ask better questions**

Let's suppose, as part of your belief system, you believed the following:

*"I attract the circumstances into my life
to be used as catalysts for my growth."*

In other words, what if you believed there was a cause/effect relationship between your thoughts, intentions and actions (as causes), and the situations you found your self in (the effects)? What if you believed your higher self—based on its desire for soul development—creates specific situations that are designed to lead you down a certain path in order to fulfill your purpose for being here?

How would having that belief affect your life? Well, for one, you would cease to believe that life is a series of random, mysterious events and situations. You would look for the order and the reason behind the things that happen. You would become more accountable for what happens in your life. You would stop blaming other people, luck or a vengeful deity for the things that happen. If you were poor, you wouldn't blame society. If you were overweight, you wouldn't blame genetics, or your metabolism, or the sugar in your food.

You would also ask different questions. If your relationship failed, you wouldn't simply blame the other person—asking "why did they do this to me?" If your job/school application was rejected, you wouldn't blame cruel fate—asking "Why me?" You would ask your self, "How did I ask for or attract this turn of events into my life?" "How is this helping me to grow?" "If, on some level, I requested this, how does this support my purpose here?" "How is this preparing me for the 'next time?' "What things do I need to modify, improve, or change about my self, my thoughts and my actions in order for things to go the way I want them to next time?"

You would see the circumstances in your life as offering clues, guidance, information and lessons for your evolution to a more enlightened state, and devote more time to changing your beliefs, thoughts and actions in order to attract and create the circumstances you desire.

You might even adopt the same mantra I use whenever circumstances in my life don't match what I say I want: *"What is the affirmative use of this apparent limitation?"*

For example, if you are sick in your quest for health; if you are judged or underestimated; if you are experiencing lack, scarcity, delay or deprivation of any kind, the question is the same: *"What is the affirmative use of this apparent limitation? How can I respond in such a way that I can transform it, evolve and/or provide some benefit to my self and others?"*

You can see how just changing one single belief about life (and acting from that belief) could have far-reaching effects on your entire experience.

With a better belief system... You produce better results

What if you believed:

"Real food consists of fruits, vegetables, nuts and grains in as close to their natural state as possible."

What if you believed the human body was designed to eat only real food, and made a decision to act on that belief and only eat real food from now on? What if you believed that anything that was an animal, or anything processed, genetically modified, grown with chemicals, fed antibiotics, sprayed with pesticides, micro-waved, colored or cooked, and that came in a box or can was unnatural, and no longer real food? You wouldn't need advertising campaigns, product manufacturers, scientists, food councils or food and drug agencies to validate your food choices. You wouldn't need anyone's permission to eat an apple. You wouldn't need the dairy council, the meat council, or fast food restaurants to tell you what was healthy and what wasn't. You would be your own authority.

As a result, you might find your self getting slimmer and healthier. You might find certain ailments reversing. You might find you are not getting as sick as often. You might gain control and mastery over your health, reduce your fear of sickness, your dependence on drugs, and ultimately stick around longer to enjoy life!

> **Living Truism:** the single, most significant obstacle to living true to your self is having an inadequate, ineffective (i.e. "wrong") belief system. The more in alignment your

> belief system is with truth, the greater degree of success you will experience in living true to your self. The more out of synch your belief system is with truth, the more failure and frustration you will experience with living true to your self.

~

You also need a better belief system, because, as is becoming increasingly evident to increasing numbers of people: everything you believe…..is wrong.

Everything you believe …is wrong!

Introduction to the Ageless Adept; applicable to all areas of life

This may come as a surprise to you, but it's entirely possible that everything you believe to be true about food, medicine, health, illness and aging is nothing more than a set of subjective ideas put forth by people who really don't have a handle on truth, don't know what they're doing, or worse, don't have your best interests at heart—people who are playing by a faulty rulebook or, worse, with no rule book at all.

Uninformed ideas, blind assumptions and outright lies underlie many of the food and (increasingly prevalent) drug commercials that air on television and radio. I'm sure you're familiar with many of these assumptions: that milk does a body good; that meat is real food for real people; that cancer can't be cured; that the common cold is inevitable; that allergies can only be relieved not ended; that hormone levels, hair growth and one's vitality inevitably decrease at certain ages; and that the drugs these companies are pushing actually heal and aren't, in fact, more dangerous than the ills they claim to cure, given the extensive list of (sometimes even fatal) side effects warned of in the disclaimers.

The sales pitches for these products start with these assumptions as "givens" and are never challenged. As a result, people buy into them (operative word "buy'), and continue a vicious cycle that ends up perpetuating the very lifestyle that caused their ills in the first place.

The society seems to have lost a vital road map and is headed in a direction of devolution that serves nothing more than to support the industries that profit from peddling the products. The products allow people to believe they can maintain their destructive lifestyles, while purchasing so-called "cures" that, in actuality, do nothing more than temporarily relieve, mask or replace the symptoms of the illnesses the lifestyles cause.

I've always lived my life with a healthy dose of skepticism towards that which most everyone else takes as true. In my own quest for truths related to health, I've met people who've actually cured lupus, sent their cancers into remission, gotten rid of their allergies, eliminated colds, and now live pain-free lives all based on truths that few are addressing publicly, or worse, truths which are ridiculed or suppressed.

For those pursuing a new paradigm of health, wellness, disease, aging and youth, what you need are:
- a set of stable truths through which to see the world anew
- a new understanding of nature that encourages new questions
- a method of critical analysis to arrive at your own answers
- a new set of possibilities and choices based on those answers
- a common sense philosophy on which to base your new lifestyle, all based on a foundation of essential truths which never change.

It contains truths you can prove for your self. And like all great truths, they don't require PhDs to comprehend. These are truths whose validity and effectiveness are accessible to just about everyone. [End of excerpt]

The preceding introduction alludes to some of the wrong and limiting beliefs—in the area of health, in particular —that attempt to control our lives. The truth—which for many people could be too frightening to accept—is that our entire belief system as it relates to health, religion, history, politics, education, life, death, money, our selves, other people, the world, the universe and how it works, are also largely based on fallacies or agendas of control. These beliefs are allowed to continue unchallenged for various reasons, and affect your ability to live true to your self.

If I believed, for example, that "milk does a body good," and acted on that belief in an effort to live true to my self in the area of my physical health, I might find my self experiencing colds, mucous, allergies, weakened bones, and cancer. I would become frustrated in my efforts to achieve health without ever knowing the real reason why.

Your mission is to strive to see beyond the constructs.

Seeing beyond the constructs

Recently, a friend and I had a discussion that had me thinking about the assumptions people make about individuals and nations often labeled as "poor" or "poverty-stricken."

This is not meant as a definitive treatise on the definition and dilemma, causes and consequences, or the solutions and salvation for these situations we call "poverty" or "prosperity." It simply offers some ideas that might allow you to step outside the common assumptions and standard paradigms to achieve new ways of looking at things.

A few thoughts about nations

As it affects nations, poverty is a condition of the environment brought about by the manipulation of economic and societal forces. A nation can be afflicted with poverty for many reasons.

Nations can become poor if their resources—human and mineral—are exploited for the benefit of another nation's prosperity.

Nations can become poor if wars are fought on their soil, and their infrastructure, as well as the will of the people are destroyed.

A nation can sink deeper into poverty if it becomes easier for it to rely on outside help than it is to become self-sufficient. (If, because of trade regulations or government subsidies for citrus farmers in one rich nation, it becomes cheaper for a poorer nation to import oranges than grow them itself, then this makes poverty and dependence more likely.)

A nation can also sink deeper into poverty if farmers are not allowed to grow and store their own seeds. For example, if they are forced—by market practices and trade regulations—to purchase the genetically-modified/owned seeds of a corporation in a prosperous country, they will rarely develop the means for their own economic independence.

In our carefully constructed, man-made society, nothing happens by accident. Everything is by design. Laws and regulations are created for a purpose and with an agenda. Think about it. If there is a natural desire and urge in humans toward survival and self-sufficiency, and if a tree will grow by simply planting a seed, then what accounts for the inability of a person and ultimately a nation, to begin to extricate itself from poverty? In other words, no nation simply arrives at a state of poverty and dependence randomly. There are always many external forces at play that one should consider in any discussion about poverty as it affects nations.

It's all a construct, my friend

When I say that something is a "construct," I simply mean it has been constructed. It is something decided and agreed upon first by a few, then by the followers in a group or society, ostensibly to ensure the survival of that group or society. Just think about what qualifies as "intelligence" "education" and "required reading" when one nation falls under the control of another. It's all just a construct, you see.

It's an idea that has been accepted and adopted as normal, but it's not necessarily the natural order of things. It's just a decision. Every distinct and separate group can decide to create and live according to a different set of constructs.

Similarly, when you talk about individual achievements of financial success within a society, there are many things that we take to be *normal*, that are, in fact, not *natural*.

Remember this: this thing we call financial success, this idea we call wealth, this aspiration we call prosperity is based on a construct that says, among other things, more is better, the earth is ours to rape and pillage, consumerism is the order of the day, we must keep getting richer and richer by any means necessary. This "infinite growth through greed" concept is an unnatural construct imposed on the masses, and on nature, by ways of thought that are not in alignment with the natural order of things. A society could just as easily choose to base civilization upon harmony, sustainability, and meeting (not exceeding) the needs of the people, as Gandhi famously said.

So, when you look at a nation that is not prosperous within this unnatural construct, and notice within that society the existence of other such circumstances as low morale, low self-esteem, inferiority complexes, educational deficits, and if you then *equate* one to the other, you may be committing a cardinal sin of analysis: equating correlation with causation. In other words, you might believe, "because these two factors exist together, one must cause the other."

Similarly, when you look at a person who is not prosperous, and then conclude that there must be something "wrong" with him or her that is causing that economic state, you are similarly using an invalid yardstick for measurement.

In fact, everything's a construct.

If, for some reason, however, you *do* want to make such assessments of better than or worse than, I suggest to you this: that the standards by which an individual or nation are often judged as desirable, valuable, worthy, good, or bad....
(a) have nothing to do with what we consider *intelligence* (because that, too, is a construct of society which determines what information is considered valuable, and which is not.)

(b) have nothing to do with what we consider *beauty* (because that, too, is a societal construct which determines what features and appearance are considered attractive, and which aren't)

(c) have nothing to do with any *fixed or objective reality*. You can choose to find and use any different means/measurements for determining what is desirable, authentic, good and bad in your world.

Remember: If it's not natural, it's a construct.

The point.

My point is that if you experience poverty, whether in your personal life, or as a nation, it has nothing to do with any inherent inferiority—there's nothing genetically wrong—in your makeup. The inability or choice not to function in a certain way and produce specific results in what is an unnatural environment, should never be used to assign value and worth to an individual, group or nation. Similarly, just because most everyone has decided to play an alien game, does not make those who are playing it, any "better" than those who do not. It just means they've decide to practice, play and master the game. But, the game itself, you see, is flawed.

Yes, the game is flawed. As I've said, this construct we call financial success, this idea we call wealth, this thing we call prosperity is based on a construct and a capitalist imperative that says, among other things, consumerism is the order of the day, more is better, the Earth is ours to rape and pillage, we must keep getting richer and richer by any means necessary. This "infinite growth through greed" concept is an unnatural construct imposed on the masses by ways of thought that are not in alignment with the natural order of things. To use a phrase that has become quite common these days: it is not sustainable.

In my conversations, I never make the mistake of saying one person is better or worse than—inferior or superior to—another simply because of his or her decision or (in)ability to produce specific results in what I believe to be an inherently unnatural system. I would never make the mistake of assigning the tag of "bad" to a nation simply because they don't appear to be going along with a particular game as decided by foreign ways of thinking. (There are some interesting books and articles about linear left-brain versus holistic right-brain ways of thinking and viewing the world that are relevant here.)

For just as poverty is *not* an indication of inferiority, neither is wealth an indication of superiority, morally or otherwise. Some of the most morally bankrupt people on the planet can, and have accumulated hoards of wealth. (In fact, some people argue that because the entire system is flawed in its underlying construct—alien to basic human nature and morally and ethically bankrupt itself—that achieving success within it necessarily requires one to manifest the same qualities. I don't believe this to be true. I believe one can survive and thrive in this construct without selling one's soul.)

But, it's no excuse

As unnatural as the construct may be, it's no excuse for poor performance. *"The test is hard, mommy, so it's OK if I fail"* wouldn't be accepted by your parents or your teachers, and it won't cut it for living true to your self. It won't cut it because there's also another law in effect: I call it the "Second Law of Passion Dynamics." This law, which was introduced in *Turn Your Passion into Profit*, says you are naturally endowed with the means for your survival. You were sent—or you chose to come—here to experience this plane of existence, and you have been given everything you need in order to function, survive and thrive.

We are all born and forced to play out an existence within this unnatural, yet powerfully constructed system. Encouragingly, many of us, at an early age, recognize the flaws, the injustices, the contradictions and lies of the system and fight against it, but then ultimately fall in line and play the game as it has been constructed.

So, if you wish to play the game, function within the system as it exists, produce certain results, and accumulate this thing called wealth, it means you will have to make a decision to act in a particular way. You have a few choices. You could

(1) simply get a job, or (2) you could harness the skills you were given in order to achieve a slightly different goal.

In theory, a job, will allow you to survive. However, I suggest option number two. I suggest you play the game by turning your passion into profit and living true to your self.

Rules of the game

If you wish to use this strategy to play the game, there are certain constructs you must dismantle, and others you must adopt especially if you are making the transition from an employee mindset, a mindset into which many of us are indoctrinated from birth.

To do this, you must first separate the connection you may have in your mind that equates your self worth with your net worth. You must also remove the belief you have that money, its acquisition and accumulation are evil. You must then accept that you have something of inestimable value inherent in you. Then you must find out what that thing of value is. Next (and this is important), you must be willing to accept money for the thing(s) of value that you offer to the world. Then, you must create a product or service based on that value. Then, you must offer that value to the world using the channels that have been created. Then you must communicate that value to increasing numbers of people.

The same general rules apply to those seeking prosperity for a nation. Of course, there are many other factors that make governing a nation toward prosperity a much more challenging task. As an outsider to this thing called politics and governance, I cannot pretend to know all the intricacies of foreign relations, domestic debt, global economic forces, treaties, budgeting and mass psychology that one must take into account to govern effectively.

However, as an outsider, I can, perhaps see more clearly that re-educating the masses and offering them a new definition of prosperity is essential. Discarding the first world definition of progress and prosperity is critical. Identifying and eliminating outside influences that seek to undermine your nation's true progress and the prosperity of your people is required. (If, while you are educating your people into a new paradigm, others are allowed to brainwash your populace with their unnatural, unsustainable and counterproductive concepts of education, beauty, food, diet, health, religion, progress and prosperity), it will be virtually impossible to extricate your nation from poverty and dependence.

The challenge

Remember, if you are like many, your current state of "success" in financial terms is being defined and dictated by an external construct. Your ability to succeed within this construct is not connected to your true worth as a living being. Furthermore, your success within this construct is entirely within your control if you decide to take the necessary steps required to play the game.

The challenge, as I see it, for both individuals as well as nations, is discovering how to play the game, survive, thrive and prosper without sacrificing things of real, authentic value. Among those things of real value I consider to be the Earth itself, it's natural beauty, your health, your right to self-sufficiency, access to land on which to live and the rights, freedom and access of others in the society to the same.

That change can only come about if you can step outside the current constructs and assumptions, see things as they really are, assess reality objectively, and then make different choices and choose different strategies that empower and free you and your nation to move from this thing we call poverty to a thing we can truly say is prosperity!

Criteria for a belief system

Now that we have a few reasons for needing a better belief system, an idea of what's wrong with the current belief system, plus a few words of warning for those embarking on a new paradigm, let's begin to develop some criteria for what a new belief system should actually accomplish. We've already established some basics. Now, let's consider some more detailed criteria.

I once read a book titled *Four Arguments for the Elimination of Television,* by Jerry Mander. When Mander wrote his book in 1978, there was no CNN, no worldwide Web, no hundreds of cable channels streaming into our homes, no iPods, no Blackberries, and no laptops. However, his insights into how the increasing influence of television affects our society are quite profound. Mander's four arguments revolve around the effects that television has had on the following:

1. The critical thinking skills of human beings.

2. Our relationship to natural environments.

3. The physical and mental health of human beings.

4. The knowledge/power balance in a democratic society.

In one section of the book, Mander lays out the pre-conditions that exist(ed)—and to which television has contributed—that have set the stage for the conditions mentioned in the four arguments. In other words, if one wished to deliberately create the deterioration of critical thinking skills, the disconnection with the natural environment, the weakening of physical and mental health, and the drastic imbalance in wealth, knowledge and power in our society, certain things need to be consciously put in place.

He begins, *"Imagine that like some kind of science fiction dictator, you intended to rule the world. You would probably have pinned over your desk a list something like this..."* He then proceeds to list the eight pre-conditions.

Now, anyone who coaches, consults or advises others on starting a business, achieving optimum health, maximizing their creative potential or changing their lives has encountered the mental and emotional blocks that exist in people's self esteem, self perception and awareness, worldview, and belief levels that prevent them from setting goals, executing their plans, and moving forward with their lives in ways they desire.

As I read each of Mander's eight pre-conditions for total control of the masses, it occurred to me that each condition to which television has contributed mirrors exactly a condition that I encounter among the people I coach. So, rather than repeat the eight pre-conditions here, I'm going to offer a prescription for how to *undo* the damage that television (and similar technologies) has done and continues to do.

8 Steps to FREE the World

To paraphrase the line from the "Pinky and the Brain" cartoon *("Same thing we do every night, Pinky: try to rule the world!")*, I'm going to take each item on Mander's list of how to *rule* the world, and by writing its opposite, offer you 8 Steps to *Free* the World! In order to free the world, you must:

1. Increase personal knowledge.

Make it easier for people to know about their selves, how they function, what a human being is, and how the human fits into the wider natural systems of the universe. This will make it possible for the human to recognize what is natural and real from what is artificial and contrived. People *can* achieve greater control of their selves, their needs, and their health, and find the answers they need on their own without the input of so-called experts and authorities from outside the self. Personal knowledge and experience is the best authority.

2. Encourage comparisons and connections.

Show people how their present lives are connected to earlier societies, older languages, and how it all fits together in historical context. Promote and foster the awareness of and respect for indigenous cultures, natural environments, and other non-human life forms.

When people see their selves in relation to and connected to other systems, they act more responsibly and with a group ethic that benefits the whole world rather than simply the individual.

3. Connect people directly with each other.

Encourage interactive, group experiences where people interact with each other rather than with an external show, presentation or performance. For example, a spectator sport or movie date is not really a group experience because while people do gather together, each person is in their own brain, simply sitting and watching something outside of the group. We want interpersonal exchange, not just a mass experience.

4. Encourage sensory experiences.

People need more sensory (sight, smell, touch, hearing, taste) experiences rather than solely mental experiences. A focus only on mental experiences separates the mind from the body and makes it harder to remain grounded in reality.

5. Encourage personal experience.

Encourage unique, individualized, experiential experience rather than pre-arranged, edited, crafted experiences. To develop a real understanding of the world, an individual must experience the world for his self or her self rather than through a produced, edited show or performance.

6. Discourage drug use and the need to "escape."

The pacifying effects of drug use, tobacco, food and sex nullify the individual's desire and motivation to take the necessary actions to change their situations. However, once many of the previous strategies are implemented, and people feel more connected and personally empowered, this need to escape will decrease.

7. Decentralize sources of information.

In some ways, the Internet is doing this by creating multiple sources of information that are competing with traditional sources. However, many people still receive what they consider to be valid, authentic, and unbiased "news" from single source entities. Information is power. It is also freedom. Once people—through social networks and websites—realize the reality they are being fed by the centralized, nightly newscasts is biased and distorted for specific agendas, they can begin to approach a degree of freedom of thought and action.

8. Redefine happiness and the meaning of life.

As a result of the advertising-driven medium of television and its cousins of radio, print and, yes, the Internet, people have developed a skewed definition of happiness. They are taught to have certain needs, taught to connect those needs with what they believe happiness to be, and are encouraged to become obedient consumers in order to satisfy those needs. The purpose of advertising and media is to create consumers who keep the wheels of the economy turning.

It is easy to teach people a skewed definition of happiness if, as a result of television, 1. They don't value their own self-acquired knowledge, 2. They see their selves as disconnected from the past and other cultures, 3. They are unconnected from each other, 4. They are deprived of sensory experiences, 5. They get their experience and interpretation of life through third parties (television anchors, talk show hosts, newspaper editors, etc.), 6. They escape into drugs, and 7. All their information comes from a single source.

However, once a person experiences the Eight Steps to Free The World, it becomes easier to introduce a new definition of happiness and the meaning and purpose of life.

What's needed in that new definition are the following:
- a definition of happiness that emphasizes expansion and growth and the achievement of one's fullest potential.
- a definition of life's purpose that focuses on uplifting and being of service to others.
- a definition of one's profession that is based on the discovery and development of one's passion and natural talents.

In addition, what we need to be taught as functions of education and maturation are:
- an interaction with one's self that focuses on developing one's creativity.
- an interaction with others that focuses on giving unconditional love.
- an interaction with the environment that is based on stewardship and not exploitation.

When you really think about it, isn't this what our formal educational system should be doing for our children? Is it not ideally what careers and jobs should offer us? Is it not ideally what our daily lives should be all about?

As you go forward with your resolutions and re-commitments to live a more prosperous life for your self and your children and to make a difference in the lives of others, consider how all the definitions, habits, perceptions and opinions we have, have been fed to us all our lives, and consequently, how caught up most of us are in an experience that has been artificially created for us.

Things need to change. So, if your life seems as if you're a laboratory rat caught in a spinning wheel, with your brain simply reacting to pre-programmed commands, then from now on when you interact with your family after work, or your children after school, or simply with your self, as you unwind from the day's activities, ask your self (and your brain) seriously, "What are we doing tonight?"

> **Living Truism:** To live true to your self, you must watch less television.

~

It bears saying that one of the things I did to live true to my self was to stop watching, and eventually give away my television. Now, may I share with you the belief system I discovered, developed and used to replace its influence?

May I suggest, therefore...?

A Better Belief System

1. The universe is perfect.
2. People are predictable.
3. There is an unseen realm.

Those three ideas form the foundation of my belief system of choice. This belief system is all I need to live the perfect life true to my self. This belief system helps me personally meet the eight-step criteria for freeing the world, starting with the freeing of my self. It just may help you as well. Let's explore each concept in depth.

FOUNDATIONAL BELIEF #1

I. The Universe is perfect

Existence implies perfection.
Therefore, nothing imperfect exists.

If I had to sum up, in a single sentence, the most important thing I've learned in life, it would be this: that the universe is perfect. Yes, the universe is perfect. That line has become my mantra, my new awareness, and the foundation upon which my belief system is based.

The case of perfection

"Perfect? The universe? How can that be?" you ask. *"With wars, famine, death, disease and all manner of apparent imperfection, how can you say the universe is perfect?"*

When I say the universe is perfect, I mean that things and events in this universe proceed by divine order, according to (some kind of) plan, that things are governed by certain knowable laws, and that, therefore, things unfold predictably. I mean that the universe is perfect in its adherence to these basic laws of reality, and that nothing imperfect—i.e. outside of the plan—can ever exist.

Knowing (and acting) on the certainty that the universe is perfect helps you seek out and identify the order in life's events. It helps you develop the best response to the things that happen to you. It empowers you, and helps you deal with and overcome adversity faster, and it can be applied to every single area of your life where there is a need for action, reaction, response or understanding.

For example, this simple belief can help you in matters of health. I recently asked a friend who was interested in eating healthy which would be better for her body, vegetables grown locally and eaten fresh, or frozen vegetables from the supermarket. She had to think about her answer for a while because she believed that the two were pretty much equivalent.

But what if she knew that the universe is perfect, then she would know that nature is perfect, and that man cannot improve on nature. She would know that anything that was NOT here at the beginning is harmful in some way. *Convenient?* Perhaps. *Efficient?* For sure. *Necessary?* Arguable. But, *more nutritious?* Unlikely.

The perfection of the universe also means something more philosophical. It goes beyond simply how you deal with nature and the physical world. It means you believe beyond the shadow of a doubt that everything that happens to you in life is actually helping you. In other words, *"The universe is perfect, so all things work towards my growth and good."*

You live in a perfect, creative and supportive universe, and everything that happens to you is moving you towards the realization of your goals and the fulfillment of your purpose and is a constant demonstration of how the universe operates in its perfection. This belief helps you interpret life's ups and downs not as the universe's attempts to keep you back, but as lessons to be learned, opportunities to be seized, and the universe's attempts to support and move you towards your goals and ideals. It's up to you to find and heed the lessons, identify the opportunities and respond accordingly.

Computer crash? What's the lesson here? House burned down? What hidden opportunity is being presented? Relationship ended? What new person am I making room for?

And here's the somewhat paradoxical kicker: You will only find the lesson, the opportunity, or that new person (the silver lining in all of life's events), if you believe it is there! It is always there, but your success in finding it will vary based on the degree of your belief in its existence.

Such a belief system has the unique property of not only empowering you to deal with every adversity, but also of being its own insurance policy! In other words, even if, conceivably, there is *no* benefit to your house burning down, your *belief* that there is a benefit keeps you focused on finding the affirmative response to the apparent limitation, empowers you to overcome the challenge, and has you expecting the good that will come your way as a result. You win either way!

Isn't that a much better response to life's situations than: *"Why do bad things always happen to me? Life doesn't want me to succeed. Life is unfair. This is terrible, woe is me?"*

Yes, everything hinges on this: that the universe is perfect. Your fulfillment raising a family, your job satisfaction, your success in business, your growth as a human being, your happiness living true to your self, all hinge on the acceptance of this single, simple, yet profound statement. Once you believe this, everything else falls into place.

So, starting today, practice repeating the mantra when faced with any seemingly unwelcome situation in your life. The moment you realize that something is happening that you consider "bad," start repeating: "The universe is perfect! The universe is perfect! The Universe is perfect!"

Similarly—and this is important, and often overlooked—you should also practice your new mantra whenever you realize something is happening that you consider "good." Doing so is an act of gratitude, which is a quality and practice necessary for your evolution and growth!

Presuppositions

In order to fully benefit from, and implement your life strategies and responses based on the belief that the universe is perfect, you must have a few supporting beliefs as well. In other words, it is easier to believe in and benefit from the perfection of the universe when:

- you believe everything and everyone including your self has a purpose here on this plane of existence.

- you have chosen to live your life in the service of others, not just in the service of self.

- you understand and respect the law of cause and effect, such that nothing that happens to you or others in life should surprise you as random or unexpected.

- you understand that the single cause of unhappiness in life is simply having an unmet expectation.

- you understand that you can't change other people, what they believe, or how they respond to you; you can only change your reactions to these things.

- you understand that the planet is going through significant changes as part of a cosmic shift in consciousness, and that we are all here at this moment in time by divine agreement to assist in the transition.

- you believe that all of this is not random; that there is a plan; we are part of its unfolding; we chose to be here.

Summary

To summarize: "We live in a perfect, ordered, creative and supportive universe, and everything that happens to us is moving us towards the realization of our goals and the fulfillment of our purpose. It's up to us to find and heed the lessons, identify the opportunities and respond accordingly."

> **Living Truism**: In order to live true to your self, you must believe that the universe is perfect.

~

If the universe is perfect; if there is order; if there is law, then it follows that some things which we may have believed were unknowable, are in fact knowable and predictable. This brings us to the *second* foundational belief of the Living True belief system.

FOUNDATIONAL BELIEF #2

II. People are predictable

There is only order here.
There are patterns.
Things are knowable.
People are predictable.

Why life seems so random

The second foundational belief of the Living True belief system is that people are predictable. I'm using the word "people" as a euphemism for life. So by this I mean there are patterns to many aspects of life (events, politics, nature, as well as people's behavior) that can be known.

There is a formula that goes like this: *"Peace of Mind" comes when persons or a society are "centered." Centeredness comes from certainty. Certainty comes from only one place: the recognition of patterns. So when a person or society has recognized a pattern as great as all of Creation, there is great certainty and centeredness—and there is great Peace of Mind.*
-from *The Mayan Calendar: The Next Nine Years*

When I read that quote, I instantly related to it because it clarified something I've been doing all my life. I realized that my mind has always been in search of patterns. It's the quest and discovery of patterns that makes me good at mathematics, and what made obtaining my civil engineering degree a bit easier. It's what helps me be an effective writer, coach, public speaker and friend. Patterns help me understand life.

Once a pattern is discerned, it can be recorded, codified, tested, extrapolated to other situations and taught as an effective means of negotiating reality. If the pattern is based on natural phenomena, it can be recreated if need be, but more importantly it can be used to understand the laws that govern the patterns. Once a pattern is recognized it means that something predictable is behind it. A predictable thing is a knowable thing. It is this knowingness that leads to certainty.

Certainty, like the certainty of having a good tip on a horse race, can help you beat the odds. Life is like that. If you know with a degree of certainty what's going to happen next, you can plan your moves, anticipate, prepare for, adjust and position your self to create the outcome you desire.

Yes, but people???

Yes. Despite what you have been led to believe, people are, in fact, predictable. The more you know about what motivates people; the more you know about what moves people to action; the more you know about how people think; the more you know about the patterns that exist in people's behavior and life choices; the more you know about how people are wired, the more they become predictable.

The following are some simple categories and classifications that, while not mainstream, have helped me recognize that predictability.

More about soul ages

Have you, or anyone you know ever been referred to as an "old soul?" It's a common expression, used to identify a person whose personality, perspective, attitudes, interests, demeanor, visage and/or aura seem to suggest that she's been here (on this planet) before. Children with apparently maturely developed interests, abilities, personality traits and even knowledge have been referred to as having or being old souls.

It would stand to reason, that if there are "old" souls, that there must also be "young" souls, and souls of every "age" in between, and in fact, there are—according to philosophers, mystics, seers and sages who, for centuries have observed, experienced or channeled information about this concept.

The concept of old and young souls is based on the idea that our immortal souls have had many different experiences on this plane of existence, and that some of us souls—in the ongoing adventure to experience all there is—have been here many times, in different identities, while other souls have had fewer "repeats" or are new to the earth school.

Whatever your views on the idea of reincarnation—an intuitively obvious fact to some, and poppycock to others—the idea that people are born with varying levels of spiritual development and maturity doesn't require any great leap in belief to appreciate. So, let's take a look at what the concept of "soul age" is all about.

Five soul ages

According to one well-known source, there are five states—or ages—of soul development: Infant, Baby, Young, Mature and Old. Each age has its own set of challenges, motivations and aspirations. Here is just a brief overview of all of them:

Infant Souls are driven by fear, and challenged with basic survival. There isn't yet much feeling for ethics or personal morality. The Infant Soul has to be taught what is right and wrong. Love or sexuality will be experienced on the level of lust.

Baby Souls are a little more comfortable in the world, less fear-driven, but require structure in order to feel comfortable in the world. They want to be directed and therefore seek out higher authorities who are willing to lay out clear rules for them. Traditions, rituals, and law and order provide a welcome sense of security. "That's the rule and that's what we'll do," is the typical thinking of a baby soul.

Young Souls, having mastered the Infant and Baby Soul issues of survival, discipline and order, are now looking to see how powerful they can become in the world. Ambition, status, independence and the ability to get what one wants out of life are the driving forces of the Young Soul stage. Seizing what the physical plane has to offer, vying to gain positions of prominence, power and great material wealth are important for young souls.

Mature Souls tend to focus less on the outer world and the material, and more on the inner world as well as relationship issues. The questions "Who am I?" and "Why am I here?" are asked with frequency in these lives. Emotions open up, boundaries between people break down. Non-traditional religions, meditation, and metaphysics start to look interesting.

Old Souls have detached from the emotional intensities of the Mature Soul period and get more objective about the ups and downs of life.

By the time a soul has arrived at the old soul stage, they've had dozens of lifetimes in varieties of cultures and classes thoroughly blended into their essences. It is much more difficult, therefore, for Old Souls to get embroiled in the right-and-wrong, us-and-them games people and countries both play. Seeing the whole picture in this way makes Old Souls calmer, more peaceful and centered. It can also make them appear passive or weak to the other soul ages.

According to the soul age belief, a being will go through different levels in each age so that by the time a person has completed a stage, they've had anywhere from seven to twenty lifetimes in that stage.

It also should be obvious that certain cultures and countries exhibit behavior consistent with different stages of soul development. So, for instance, a country like the United States is evidently more driven by a young soul mentality than a country like Holland or Sweden.

Soul age knowledge applied

So, how do you apply this to living true to your self?

Knowing that an individual's and even an entire nation's interests and attitudes can be defined and understood in terms of a soul age gives you a bit of an advantage over other people who believe that behavior is strictly a function of biological age, race or gender (soul age cuts across all these lines), or that wiring can be changed by affirmations alone (Yes, they can be helpful, but no amount of self help technique will ever get an old soul to define her self by the kind of watch she wears.).

Although there are similarities in behavior and attitudes between biological age and soul age, there is no direct correlation. In other words, a 90-year-old person could be a young soul, and an 18-year-old could be an old soul, exhibiting the attitudes and behavior unique to that respective soul age.

Similarly, no group, society or nation is made up entirely of people of a single soul age. You will find old souls and baby souls in every country.

However, what the concept of soul age can do is equip you to understand and deal more effectively with people. Politicians know, for example, that they can "sell" their ideas with different levels of success in different regions of the country based on the soul age of that region. Marketers know that certain movies or products, for instance, will sell better in certain countries because of the prevailing soul age of that country. It's difficult to sell luxuries in a country whose population is at the infant stage preoccupied with survival. Similarly, it is easier to sell status symbols of wealth and achievement in a country operating at a young soul age.

The soul of the self

However, an even deeper, more compelling, and ultimately more useful reason for becoming familiar with the soul age concept has to do with self-knowledge. Knowing your own soul age can make many things clearer for you. It can explain a lot about who you are and why you do what you do. It can help you understand why certain things have always attracted or repelled you. It can help you see the patterns underlying the choices you've always felt compelled to make throughout your life. It can help you feel more comfortable with who you are, and who you have come to be.

It can also help you understand why your best efforts to become someone different have always produced the same results. You might finally recognize that you are an old soul, for instance, and like most old souls, not interested in social entanglements, restrictive corporate culture, political arguments and anything that drives, say, a young soul. Or, you might recognize your self as a young soul driven to succeed at all costs, and to make things happen, and that the old soul traits you wish you had, of being calm and easygoing and going with the flow, just aren't part of your soul's makeup. Yes, knowing your soul age might just bring some peace of mind and acceptance of who you are into your existence.

At the same time, accepting your soul age should not be an excuse for not attempting to grow and change.

In essence, the more you know about who you are, and the purpose you came here to achieve, the easier it will be to craft a lifestyle, a career, and even a business that is in alignment with, and that offers the greatest fulfillment for the deepest parts of your self. Live true to your soul!

Life themes, personality types, etc.

I've covered the details of life themes and personality types in "What is the SELF," so I won't repeat them here. The point, as indicated above, is the more you know about your self, the more you also learn about others. The more you learn about others, the less mysterious and random they appear, and the more predictable they become.

Event patterns and natural law

There are also knowable patterns to nature, circumstances and world events as well. There's a work known as the Kybalion that offers seven principles that are said to form the basis of hermetic philosophy. They include:

I. The Principle Of Mentalism.
II. The Principle Of Correspondence.
III. The Principle Of Vibration.
IV. The Principle Of Polarity.
V. The Principle Of Rhythm.
VI. The Principle Of Cause And Effect.
VII. The Principle Of Gender.

For instance, according to Law of Rhythm:

"Everything flows, out and in; everything has its tides; all things rise and fall; the pendulum-swing manifests in everything; the measure of the swing to the right is the measure of the swing to the left; rhythm compensates.

There is always an action and a reaction; an advance and a retreat; a rising and sinking. This is in the affairs of the Universe, suns, worlds, men, animals, mind, energy, and matter. This law is manifest in the creation and destruction of worlds; in the rise and fall of nations; in the life of all things; and finally in the mental states of Man…"

Imagine how much more predictable events, as well as people's actions would be if you knew that such actions were governed by certain natural laws known for the ages, and you actually knew what those laws were! As a public domain text, the Kybalion is freely available on the Internet for you to examine. (See appendix for a summary, and download at www.waltgoodridge.com)

.

Yes. People.

Without such critical understandings, everything *does* seem quite random, inexplicable and even chaotic. Think, however, how all the seemingly premature deaths, war, crime, poverty, and the presumably random illnesses, and apparent handicaps that afflict people would be interpreted if you believed that we chose to be here, chose what themes we wanted to experience, and even chose our "exit points" once our purpose was served? It would explain a lot.

You would see people for who and what they have chosen to be, and accept that choice, with all its highs and lows, while you focus on your own. You might see fear and evil intent in people's actions as they live out there own life themes, but you wouldn't see chaos in the unfolding, so you don't rail against things happening the way they do or wonder why people don't all think and act the same.

You'd realize that everyone has a theme they are living out, something they have chosen to express, and so, you would no longer expect the "gurus" to be "catalysts," nor the "warriors" to be "healers," nor the "pawns" to be "leaders."

Essentially, your expectations would change. People would become predictable. You would see your own place in the grand scheme through different eyes. You could more effectively pursue your reason for being here because you would see the order behind it. It would explain some of the patterns in your life. You'd realize that you attract circumstances in your life to be used as "catalysts" for your growth and the fulfillment of your life theme.

The perfection of the universe, combined with these people patterns and natural laws, means that the builder will always have reason to build. The teacher will have his students. The leader will have her followers. Those who are here to rescue will, by the principles of Polarity, and Cause and Effect, find those who need to be rescued, and so it goes, because the universe is perfect, and people *are* predictable.

> **Living Truism**: In order to live true to your self, you must believe that people are predictable.

~

The reason I am even aware of these non-mainstream views of people and events, is because of the third and final component of my better belief system. It stands to reason that in order to fill in the blanks in our understanding of the universe and its perfection, and to fill in the blanks in our understanding of the predictability of people and events, one must leave room for the unseen.

FOUNDATIONAL BELIEF #3

III. There is an unseen realm

*Miracles are the norm. Other forms of life exist.
Energy is real. There are multiple planes of reality.
We exist simultaneously on these planes. Time is non-linear.
There is an invisible game.*

The reason the universe seems flawed and imperfect, the reason why people behave in ways that seem to defy normal standards of kindness, morality, ethics and even logic is not because life is bad, men are all evil, or because things are random and beyond our knowing. It's simply because we don't know the real game that's being played.

The Invisible Game

If you believe this game called life is only about what's *visible*, then many of life's questions will have answers that make little sense, and that don't maintain any degree of consistency that can be used to understand reality.

People ask *why is there war? Why do infants die? Why is there pain and suffering in the world? Why are the saviors always taken away? Why is there famine and sickness? Why do people behave the way they do?*

However, people are often taught that many such of life's questions have only visible answers. They are offered seemingly logical, plausible or scientific reasons to explain the events leading up to a war, for example, or taught concepts like crib death, assassination theories, global market economics, or given astute psychological analyses of childhood scars and emotional disturbances as being the roots of people's personalities or antisocial behavior.

However, when people ask "why" what they're usually asking is *what's the divine plan behind it all?* They are, in fact, intuitively seeking what I call the invisible game, but are often encouraged to look only at what's accessible by the five senses, while dismissing everything else as mystery, paranormal or "conspiracy theory."

I suggest to you that there is, in fact, a different game—an invisible game—being played. It is a game with a set of rules that is going to require a great deal of courage to accept. Accepting these new rules will mean uprooting your current beliefs; it will mean living with the realization that you've been lied to; that your parents, priests, politicians, and professors—though not responsible for it—are collaborators in the perpetuation of the lie; that you will be perceived as crazy, and that you may be branded a heretic, dissenter and subversive for living true to and promoting your new beliefs.

These invisible beliefs are not new ideas. They exist in many shapes and forms in a variety of texts (old and new), and are held and propagated through various worldviews, curricula, belief systems and observations.

In fact, many ideas people label as self-help, personal development, new age, new thought, quantum energy, etc., are introducing people to these "new" (previously invisible) ways of thinking, being and behaving that are more in alignment with the real game. As our global consciousness and awareness evolves, more people are being introduced to snippets of truth once considered on the "fringe," that are allowing them to live more productive, fulfilling and purposeful lives.

The truth is, life *can* be mastered. As we learned in the previous section, there are things you could choose and prove to believe that will help the world make sense to you. There are things you could choose to believe that would make things predictable to such a degree it might astound you. It might even seem you can predict the future. Yes, hidden within this invisible game is the power and peace of mind you seek!

Mastering life is just like mastering anything else. If you understand how a car works and know the rules of the road, you can be a better driver. If you understand money, and the rules of business, you can build a profitable venture. If you understand what your partner likes, you can be a better lover. If you understand life, truth and self, you can live true.

A List of Ten

Now then, I am going to offer a short list of ten ideas that exist in this unseen realm. They span a range of subjects from politics to religion to education to health. They are:

1. Hidden agendas abound
2. Human beings were seeded. We are not of this planet.
3. UFOs exist, and contact has already been made.
4. The moon is an artificial satellite that was moved into place.
5. Wars are started to make money.
6. We choose our parents and our paths before we are born.
7. Fluoride is a dangerous chemical and should not be ingested.
8. The pyramids were created by an alien race.
9. Time travel is possible.
10. It is possible to see the future, through both mechanical as well as intuitive means.

Now, here's a test. What were your initial thoughts upon reading the above list of ten? Did you say,
- Yeah, I believe it, too!
- He could be right, I don't know.
- Okay, he's gone of the deep end. Crackpot!"

Your response is what's important here. You see, I'm not asking you to believe any of these things. I am suggesting that you cannot be 100% sure that they *aren't* in the realm of possibility. In fact, scholarly books, papers, theses and documentaries have been written or created about each of these topics, proving each one true. However, if you are rigid in your refusal even to entertain them as possible, then that rigidity may extend to other areas of your life and may prevent you from living true to your self.

Again, you will find no debate here as to whether they are true or not. I suggest to you, however, that leaving room for the unseen is a good strategy for living true to your self.

> **Living Truism:** In order to live true to your self, you don't have to believe everything that I believe, but neither should you be closed to the possibility of their validity.

The magic and mystery of the unseen realm

There are an infinite number of such "List of Ten" beliefs that comprise what I call "the unseen realm" that, if they became mainstream, would challenge existing power and control. Everything from reincarnation to the existence of life on other planets, to the reason for seemingly premature deaths, to the real cause of birth defects, all exist as part of a belief system that offers plausible explanations where no explanations seem to exist. They explain what others believe is beyond knowing. In many cases, the adoption of these and other beliefs has the benefit of reducing fear, uncertainty, confusion and dependency, while increasing confidence, independence, and faith by making sense of the visible game.

However, as stated, what's more important than the actual beliefs, is your willingness to leave room for them in your assessment of reality. Simply believing there may be forces at work, of which you have no clue, that may be the real determinants of the outcomes of everything that you do is an empowering decision. This is different than believing that there is someone or something that is *controlling* the outcome. These unseen forces are marshaled at *your* command. They are consistent with the laws of the universe. Even if you do not know what these forces and laws are, they will still work for you because they are in alignment with the truth of reality.

In my own life, after seeing and experiencing countless times how money comes when needed, how the right people appear at just the right moment, how events play out in divine orchestration, and in perfect sequence and timing to move me forward towards my desires, it has become expected, and almost predictable.

As I've said before, when you commit to live true to your self, you become an agent of change, and an agent of truth. As you grow in your commitment to truth, truth becomes more of your ally, and all the miracles, magic and mystery that go along with truth are activated for your benefit and become yours to use on your behalf and for others.

Did you get that? When you live true to your self, and align your every waking thought and action with the truths of reality, there will be unseen forces that are activated which rush to your aid to support you. People will assist you. Circumstances will benefit you. You may even come to expect such manifestations as both validation of and reward for living your life in accordance with truth. Some might call it magic. You will call it living true.

> **Living Truism**: In order to live true to your self, you must believe (and eventually will come to know) that there is an unseen realm.

My summary of the unseen realm

There is divine order despite appearances. There are agendas afoot of which we are not aware. There are things to which we are blind, that have more influence on our lives than we are led to believe. We have untapped potential and abilities that lie beyond the fringes of our everyday understanding. There are truths about who we are which are unrecognized, overlooked and sometimes purposely suppressed.

I suggest that in order to live true to your self, you must embark or re-commit your self to a belief in and quest for that unseen realm. Again, some of the beliefs been branded and stigmatized as being impossible, outlandish, or subversive.

The payoff, however, is that these beliefs will help you understand the invisible game. And when you understand the invisible game, the visible game gets a lot easier. If you can anticipate what's about to happen, you can be pre-emptive in your actions. If you understand where to look for answers, then you can never be lost for too long. If you recognize where your power exists, you can tap into it and get on with the real game for which you came: to live true to your self.

What it required

Having made the choice to live from these beliefs, and their resultant understanding of reality, I now see evidence to support them everywhere I look. However, it didn't happen overnight. My own conviction as well as the outward manifestations that the universe is perfect, that people are predictable, and that there is an unseen realm, demanded patience and required a process.

I first had to make a decision. I had to decide that I wanted a different life, a better life, a more fulfilling life, a life that was not limited by history, by fear, by hatred, intolerance or what others believed was possible. As the pathway to that new life, I invested and immersed my self in personal growth.

Then, it took years of open-mindedness, of affirmations and positive self-talk. It required a commitment to internalize and apply the teachings of dozens of self-help, motivational, inspirational, philosophical, metaphysical books and audiotapes. It required attending lectures, courses and workshops on personal transformation. It required the determination to live according to a new set of principles. As I walked the path, there would be certain occurrences that provided evidence and proof of the truth and validity of the path I was on, and from which I gained encouragement to continue believing. It required the patience to keep practicing the new ways until I saw those principles fully and more predictably and reliably manifested and validated in my life.

> **Living Truism**: In order to live true to your self, you must be committed for the long haul.

Summary of The Foundational Beliefs

The Universe is perfect
People are predictable
There is an unseen realm.

So, there you have them: the three foundational beliefs of my "better" belief system.

Any belief system that creates fear, sanctions intolerance, dependence, passivity and weakness and that has you relinquish your personal power is doing you a disservice. It is my opinion, as I mentioned earlier, that the purpose of ANY belief system should be to help you see and interpret reality correctly, understand your role within it, make better survival decisions, grow, be of service to the community and connect you to your higher self to express your greatest potential and power. This belief system has the potential to do just that when applied correctly.

As you take this new belief system with you on your journey through life, people will still attack you. Obstacles will beset you. Things won't always go the way you think they should. Accidents will happen. People will meet with seemingly untimely fates. Planets will warm. Injustice will be rampant. Poverty will continue. Greed will abound. Industries will fall. Empires will collapse. Things will change. Tires will go flat. Dishes will break. Money will be lost.

However, you won't be overcome by fear or confusion. You are in sync with perfection. Rather than seeing these as negatives, you will see them as reminders of why you chose to be here at this time.

In these occurrences, you will see your own and others' life themes being played out. You will recognize how your and other people's tightly held expectations lead to unhappiness. You will recognize seemingly disastrous events as catalysts for your growth. You will see the law of cause and effect in action, and, as a result, you will seek, and invariably find, the reasons why you attracted certain events into your life, and the lessons that your higher self is constantly offering you through these events. You will see how your attachment to material things is constantly being tested. You will see how edifices built on lies inevitably fall. You will recognize the hand of angels orchestrating the pace of events in your life making sure you never arrive too soon or too late for your scheduled appointment with your higher calling. You will recognize the unseen realm of divine order, and natural law that permeates everything. You will take it all in stride, and you will know, beyond doubt...that the despite how things appear to others, that Universe is perfect, that people are, in fact, predictable, and that somewhere, somehow, wielding influence in your life, there is an unseen realm.

Part FOUR-B
Personally

> What a man believes may be ascertained not from his creed, but from the assumptions on which he habitually acts.
> ~ George Bernard Shaw

My personal beliefs

Here is a short list of some additional personal beliefs derived from those three foundational beliefs. They are culled from my experiences, education, investigation, inquiry as well as intuition, and cover matters of natural law, health, money, politics, the nature of reality, love, people, personal safety, and my purpose on the planet.

Here, then, is what I believe about my self, about people and about the universe:

About my self...

I believe...

I am here to prove a point

I believe I am here for a particular purpose. I believe I am here to tell a story. I believe that the story I am here to tell is the story of my own life. I believe the purpose of that story is to inspire, empower and equip others to grow.

I believe, too, that part of my mission and role is to stand as testament to, and be a living example of the thoughts and actions which lead to empowered change. In other words, I am here to live the life of my dreams simply to show others it can be done. This life shall question what I believe is real, and challenge what I believe about my self, about others, about the world and about the universe I live in. In this life I shall walk where others believe there is no footing; I shall act where there is no script; I shall take risks without the assurance of success.

Here's how it works: The quest for my own enlightenment and happiness puts me on a path and attracts certain experiences which I then document for the benefit of helping others to do the same or something similar. I am here to live an experience, process it, analyze it, explain it and teach it to others in the form of my own story.

I believe...

Everything counts

Have you ever noticed how often some celebrity or public figure seems to self-destruct? One minute they're flying high, a media darling, and the next, some allegation surfaces, photographs appear, and the fall from grace is swift and brutal.

To be fair, there can be any number of reasons for this. Celebrities are often easy targets for extortion. Many are framed. Allegations are often fabricated. There could be different agendas afoot to discredit or destroy being executed by those who are jealous, or who seek a financial payday.

However, in other cases, what happens is that the person's inconsistencies, hypocrisy or poor decisions catch up to them. They learn too late that actions have consequences; that somebody may be watching; that everything counts.

I'm not a celebrity, but I've always lived my life with this haunting belief that at some time in the future, I was going to be famous for extolling a certain standard of behavior. I've had visions of my self at a press conference advocating a certain ethical code or lifestyle. As such, I have to be sure that no photos of me eating a hamburger would ever show up at that press conference! I don't want documents or other evidence that shows I did anything that contradicted who or what I claimed to be. It's a funny quirk, perhaps, but I've always acted as if everything counts.

Perhaps it's a bit unrealistic to ask a college student to behave in ways that anticipate who or what she'll be in ten or twenty years. Perhaps that's too much discipline, restraint and self-control to ask of the average person. Perhaps. But then, perhaps living true to the self is not for the average person.

I believe... **Everything is connected**
The way I do ONE thing is the way I do ALL things

Draw a circle. Imagine that you are inside that circle and the circle represents your comfort zone. All that you're comfortable doing exists inside the circle, and everything you're afraid to do—your fears—exists outside the circle. By running towards a specific fear, you stretch the boundary of the circle, and the *entire* circle gets bigger, and what was once outside the circle is now on the inside, and the new you is now defined by a larger circle that includes more abilities <u>all around</u>. You are now living within an expanded comfort zone.

Any progress in *any* direction made in the conquest of your fears, expands you as a person and has effects in other areas of your life that you cannot now imagine. It doesn't matter what the fear is. It doesn't matter if it appears to be connected to your goal or not. Everything is connected.

Conquering your fear of public speaking, your fear of swimming, your fear of driving, your fear of cooking a meal for your self, expands you as a person and makes you courageous in other areas of your life well.

In particular, embracing the people you dislike or who you think dislike you will open up new doors of opportunity for you. It's been said that if you dislike someone, it's really because they remind you of something about your self that you don't like. Embracing and analyzing the flaws and faults you perceive in others is the best way to understand your self and grow personally. Find ways to reach out, work with them and share common goals and ideas. Everything inside you might be screaming "no way!" right now. That's the fear shouting.

I believe that if I can find the courage to face my fears, run towards them, meet them head on, and do the very thing that I fear the most, I believe that this affects my success in every other area of my life, because everything is connected!

I believe...

I am a channel

I once had the unique experience of being on a bus in Maryland and having one of my life rhymes* come to me fully formed, rhyme perfect, meter perfect, so quickly that I had to write double time just to keep up with its creation; as if it was being dictated to me. I've had similar creative experiences that confirm for me something that I once read: that there is only one artist, one painter, one poet, and we are all channels for her work. Because I believe that my work serves a purpose, and that I am divinely guided, then what I do as a writer/creator is simply "allow" these creations to take form and manifest here on this plane for the benefit of others. I believe, therefore, that there is a perfect flow and sequence of words, a single layout for my websites, etc. that will achieve the intended goal. I simply remain clear as a channel and allow the perfection to seek expression through me. I'll take credit with my name as author, but, between you and me, I know the truth.

[*See #59 at www.liferhymes.com for the one that stands out!]

I believe... ## My age is my #1 secret

I don't tell people my age. Here's why.

Perceptions create expectations. Expectations are thoughts. Thoughts have power. The way people perceive me affects how they relate to me. When people interact with me, their thoughts send energy towards me. I want my interactions with people free of the taint of any energy caused by thoughts that contain associations and judgments, beliefs and expectations about what it means to be of a certain age. Of course, border agents and immigration officers have access to that information, but everyone else I meet is not allowed in. That includes friends, girlfriends, even relatives who may not know exactly when I appeared on the planet.

For similar reasons, I rarely reveal what I do for a living when I meet new people on my nomad journeys. I've seen the changes in people's interaction with me once they discover I've written a few books. (Fortunately, even with the publication of this, my twentieth book, I can be assured that when I travel into the mountains of Tibet, I'll be just another anonymous stranger.) Here, too, I want an authentic interaction based simply on camaraderie, warmth, chemistry and not any intimidation or pretense based on assumed status, educational background, or perceived celebrity. Thoughts have power.

I believe... ## I don't have to respond

One of the most freeing and liberating things I learned in my life was that I don't have to respond to a question simply because it is asked. Many people feel pressured, and end up revealing things they'd rather not reveal because they don't feel empowered to say, simply, *"Sorry, I'm not going to answer that question. Sorry, that's a secret. Sorry, I never share that information. No comment. Let's talk about something else, shall we?"* or *"If you don't stop asking me that question, I'm going to walk away."*

I believe... ## I am special

That's what grandma told me, and I'm not one to argue.

I believe... ## I can do the impossible

I can do what others say cannot be done. This, of course, goes hand in hand with a belief that the universe is perfect, a belief in magic and miracles, and that I'm special. For the record, miracles are only considered to be miracles by those who don't know truth.

I believe... ## I am protected

Because I believe in an unseen realm; because I believe I am here on a mission, I believe that my safety is assured. I believe that I will be intuitively as well as overtly guided to make the best choices, and choose the best paths. I believe, that even though I may walk through the valley of the shadow of death, that I am protected.

I believe... ## I live above the fray

I make it a point to keep my self above the pettiness that often comes with being human. Not because I think I'm better than anyone else, but simply because I don't waste energy on non-productive activities. Money. Ego. Competition. Jealousy. I've learned to simply walk away. I live above it.

I believe... ## I am here to help with the transition

Two people are sitting in a doctor's waiting room. One turns to the other and says, "So, why are you here?" The other replies, "I'm here to help with the transition." It's perhaps a bit of dry humor that only old souls, light workers and metaphysicians will get, but I say that to say this:

As I mentioned earlier, choosing to believe the universe is perfect *"presupposes that you understand that the earth is going through changes as part of a cosmic shift that is occurring, and that we are all here at this moment in time by divine agreement to assist in the transition."*

This belief is always at the forefront of my mind.

I believe... **I will survive**

During a recent nomadpreneur adventure through Asia, I ended up on the island of Hainan, China, just a few days before Chinese New Year. As it is a favorite tourist getaway for people from all over the world, hotel space in Hainan during that time of year is at a premium (often 4 to 5 times the regular price), that is, if you can find an empty room. I reserved a room at a hostel, but would have to leave a day before New Year's Eve because my room had been booked way in advance by others. I knew this going into the deal.

In response to my blog post about the situation, a friend commented via email, *"Hainan on New Year's Eve??? But then, my resources are not as deep as yours."*

I replied, *"That's not depth, my friend, that's optimism."*

In the previous section, I spoke about the magic and mystery that comes with having the right belief system. I can take what others may consider risks (or mistakenly assume to be well-funded excursions) because I have faith in my resourcefulness, I am not attached to any particular outcome, I expect there are unseen forces that will be activated on my behalf, and I know, therefore, beyond a shadow of a doubt that something will come along. I know I will survive.

I believe... **I am my own authority**

I don't need anyone's permission, approval or agreement to believe the things I believe. I don't need studies to validate things that I can experience and prove for my self. I am my own authority. I don't need the evening news to tell me if eating an apple a day is good for me. I already know that the universe is perfect, that man cannot improve on nature, that everything we need for our health and well-being was here way before men in lab coats appeared with their linear minds.

I believe in... **Immortality**

I believe in immortality. I don't mean the immortality of living on in the memories of others. I mean I believe that the human beings, occupying the bodies we do here on this plane, can make a choice to remain here indefinitely—past the time frame that conventional expectations deem as a life-span.

About other people...

About people, I believe... **People are basically good**

Yes, I believe the world is essentially good; that people are basically good and kind, and that, when given the opportunity and the environment to do so, will be fair and just in their dealings. I also believe, however, that upbringing, training, circumstances, culture, and/or a belief in the lack of viable options can bring out the opposite behavior in people.

About people, I believe in... ## The Law of Obligation
People will do what people will do

Another liberating realization I made in my years of personal growth is that people will not always act or react in the ways I wish them to. In other words, the world is under no obligation. As I said before, I call it *Walt's Law of Obligation*.

Walt's Law of Obligation says: "There ain't none!"

This may be a tough lesson to learn, but people aren't obligated by *your* sense of right and wrong, to do what *you* want them to, just because *you* think it should be so, or because you've done something and expect something in return.

We live in a society where we hope everyone will adhere to the same standards of conduct. We hope people will say "please" and "thank you." We hope others will take our concerns seriously, hold up their end of a bargain, return our calls on time, pay back what they owe, allow us to merge into traffic, hold the door open for us, treat us as we treat them and so on. Yes, in our daily interactions with others, we hope people will play along with our game plan. The truth is, however, these are just expectations of what others should do.

And remember what we know about expectations? Unhappiness is nothing but an unmet expectation. The only reason anyone on this planet is unhappy is because they have an expectation of how things should be that was not met.

Can you accept that others will do as they please? Can you still keep smiling when you don't get your way? Can you give up the victim game and stop waiting for someone to treat you in a specific way? If you can, you might find life's road a little less bumpy and less aggravating. At the very least, you'll spend less time wallowing in self-pity and wondering why. This doesn't mean you'll accept abuse. Don't allow your self to be taken advantage of. Remove your self from destructive people and situations as soon as possible. At the same time, you don't have to *lower* your expectations of people either. Simply detach your self from any specific outcome. You might be surprised how liberating it might be!

About people, I believe in.... **Keeping a short list**

As I've said, I am very vigilant about who I spend time with. I have similar criteria for friends, lovers and business partners. How do I feel while and after being with them? Do they bring out the best in me? Do I feel drained and depressed, or do I feel energized and inspired? Do they whine and complain, or do they offer ideas and solutions? I am wary of people who argue on behalf of their own, or my limitations and who encourage dependence rather than independence. I keep company with people who are going in their own positive direction, or who, at the very least are not discouraging me from going in mine. I keep a short list of close friends.

About people, I believe... **People are fertilizer**

People are fertilizer for my personal growth.

One of the most helpful attitudes I've developed over the years has been how to interpret, respond to, and roll with the unexpected situations that arise in life. This secret has been expressed in many ways by different people. The essence of it, however, is that everything that happens to you, through the situations and people you encounter in life, present opportunities for you to grow spiritually and emotionally.

People will often do things that upset you, anger you, disappoint you or make you cry. The key to moving forward is to remember that every one of these situations has been orchestrated to strengthen you or to teach you something. The people who "get under your skin" have been attracted into your life with a lesson for you.

It's been said that you only get angry with a person when you encounter something in that person that mirrors something about your self that you are unhappy with. Therefore, the opportunity in every situation that angers you is that you can then identify and change an aspect of your self that the person you are angry with is bringing to the surface.

Are you angry at someone's rudeness, lack of courtesy, spitefulness? It's a sure sign they are simply reflecting a part of your self you need to grow through. Ask your self: "I'm mad at John, but what part of my own personality is John reflecting? Where in my life am I the same way with other people?Now, the converse is also important. Think about this. Have you ever been in a situation in which someone did something to you, and all your friends asked, "Doesn't that make you angry?" but you didn't actually feel anything?

The fact that you could just blow it off, walk away, forget about it, or even forgive them, is a sure sign that there was no real reflection of your self coming from that person. You were beyond the pettiness they displayed, and so they weren't pushing buttons because there were no buttons to push.

Just like the manure or fertilizer that farmers use to make their crops grow faster, people and the things they do, can serve the same purpose in your life. So, from now on, when you find your self being royally ticked off by someone, just smile and remind your self: "He's nothing but fertilizer!"

About people, I believe... **"They" are not like us**

And there are some, however, who are not like the rest of us at all, however much we wish to believe that they are.

About the universe...

While my "Better Belief System" contains a more complete overview of my beliefs about the universe, here are a few for emphasis.

About the universe, I believe in... **Order despite appearances**

If the universe is perfect, then there is order despite appearances. There are answers despite apparent mystery. There are reasons things happen the ways they do.

About the universe, I believe... **There's a formula for everything**

There's always a way to get from here to there.

About the universe, I believe... **Nothing stays the same**

Things are either expanding or contracting. Things are either improving or deteriorating. Things are either rising or falling. Things are either getting better or getting worse. This applies to people, events and the universe at large. Knowing this can help you understand life and make better decisions. Anything that appears to be staying the same, but that is definitely not getting better, is actually getting *worse*.

Think about a significant relationship in your life about which you are unsure of how to proceed. Assuming that nothing stays the same, when you think about it over the span of the last year or so, is the relationship getting better or getting worse? Your honest response will help you decide what to do.

My summary of my beliefs

These beliefs about my self, about others and about the world and universe I live in, help me remain focused, stay positive, keep motivated, act in accordance with my values and ethical code, roll with the punches, recognize opportunities, overcome obstacles, interpret setbacks, decipher clues, keep my own counsel, moderate my responses to outside influences, expect the best outcomes, and produce the results I desire. They help me live true to my self.

Living Truism: What you choose to believe about your self, about others, about the world, and about the universe result in a belief system that will either help or hinder you from living true to your self. Choose wisely.

Part FIVE

Personality

"Leadership consists not in degrees of technique, but in traits of character." ~ Lewis Lapham

The Personality Traits

Here is a short list of the personality traits, qualities and abilities I recognize in my self that I believe are vital and necessary in order to live true to my self.

I value... **The usual suspects**

Every self-help, inspirational, motivational, life altering, thought bending, view changing, personal development, success strategy book or course offers a variety of personal qualities and traits necessary for success. They are all valuable. I believe, as do most people, that you need patience, tolerance, determination, kindness, courage, faith, the ability to take risks, and so on, in order to be productive, successful, prosperous, happy, rise to the level of your greatest potential, and live true to your self. I believe that every day these qualities are brought to bear; tested if they are found weak, and rewarded if they are found strong. Yes, I believe the "usual suspects" of desirable traits are essential.

A vital personality trait is... **Discipline**

As mentioned in the Living True Test #1, the first quality that comes to mind when I think about what it takes to live true to my self is discipline. Discipline is the ability to continue on a course of action, to do the necessary thing, again and again, to reach the desired goal previously set, even when the desire, interest and commitment to reach that goal is no longer there. I've heard someone define "commitment" in similar terms. To me, however, commitment doesn't quite capture the essence of what is required. Commitment often seems to have a forced component to it. Discipline evokes more of an active and willing participation in the scenario.

It required discipline to wake up at 3:00 am (the time of day I work best) day after day to finish writing this book. It required discipline to continue writing my life rhymes, week after week for the nine years that *Walt's Friday Inspirations* ran, or my newspaper column week after week for five years. It required discipline to keep doing my radio show week after week, to trudge through the snow every Thursday night with 50 vinyl records in tow, ride the New York City buses and three subway trains to make it to the studio on time, do my one-and-a-half hour show, and then repeat the journey back home, and still have to go to work at my civil engineering job later that morning.

However, discipline alone is not enough to live true to my self. In fact, the discipline, and the ability to act might be in jeopardy if I did not also have a complementary perspective and trait that help me focus and sustain that discipline.

> **Living Truism:** It is easier to summon the discipline for a project that is fueled by your passion.

A vital personality trait is... **Long time perspective**

The first trait that helps me sustain discipline is what I call a long time perspective. That simply means that I realize that all my actions today are creating the vision I have of my self tomorrow. As I proceed on any course of action towards a goal, I am focused on the future outcome I am creating. What I am doing is building something grand. I am building something that takes time. It's not just patience. It's patience with a vision.

> **Living Truism:** It's easier to maintain a long time perspective when you are in control of how you spend your days.

A vital personality trait is... **Perseverance**

The second complementary trait that works in conjunction with having a long time perspective is the quality of perseverance.

Here is a little quiz that I always recall and share with others to help develop the right understanding of what one is building on a day-to-day basis.

Which would you rather have: a penny doubled each day for a month or $10,000? If you haven't already encountered this question, you might be tempted to take the $10,000. After all, $10,000 is $10,000, and a penny is only a penny. Even if you suspect that doubling a penny each day might in fact amount to a huge number, you might not realize just how much is really at stake. The correct answer—provided you want the option that will make you richer—is to take the penny option. Here's what you will receive each day for thirty days if you do:

Day 1 - 1 cent	Day 16 - $327.68
Day 2 - 2 cents	Day 17 - $655.36
Day 3 - 4 cents	Day 18 - $1,310.72
Day 4 - 8 cents	Day 19 - $2,621.44
Day 5 - 16 cents	Day 20 - $5,242.88
Day 6 - 32 cents	Day 21 - $10,485.76
Day 7 - 64 cents	Day 22 - $20,971.52
Day 8 - $1.28	Day 23 - $41,943.04
Day 9 - $2.56	Day 24 - $83,886.08
Day 10 - $5.12	Day 25 - $167,772.16
Day 11 - $10.24	Day 26 - $335,544.32
Day 12 - $20.48	Day 27 - $671,088.64
Day 13 - $40.96	Day 28 - $1,342,177.28
Day 14 - $81.92	Day 29 - $2,684,354.56
Day 15 - $163.84	Day 30 - $5,368,709.12

Seen for what it is, this example is truly astounding! A single penny, doubled for an entire month yields a final day's return of over 5 million dollars, and a total accumulated return of over 10 million! And notice that even by day number 15, halfway through, still nothing much appears to be happening. Yet just a little more perseverance will soon pay off.

It's an example of growth that progresses not arithmetically (i.e. by single units) but by Geometric Progression. A geometric sequence or a geometric series is a sequence of numbers where each term after the first is found by multiplying the previous term by a fixed number called the common ratio—like the progression of rewards on the popular game show *Who Wants To Be A Millionaire*, which goes from $100 to a $1,000,000 in just twelve questions by roughly doubling each prize (common ratio=2),

I always refer to this in my own life when nothing seems to be happening in the pursuit of my goals. I remind my self that little perseverance can lead to huge rewards!

> **Living Truism**: It is easier to persevere when your goals in life are of your own choosing.

A vital personality trait is... **Endurance**

Endurance is perseverance under stress. Endurance is perseverance when the reserves are practically depleted. I always remind my self and others that no matter how tired you are, bone-weary, and on your last ounce of strength—if someone approached you at that very instant and offered you ten million dollars to run a mile, you would find and pull the energy from somewhere deep inside to get the job done! Well, there might not be a guaranteed ten-million dollar prize in the equation at any given moment, but I believe those hidden reserves are always there for me to tap into at will.

> **Living Truism**: It is easier to find the both the physical and mental stamina to endure when your body and brain are healthy and free of toxins.

A vital personality trait is... **Tolerance for discomfort**

When we were young, my cousins and I played "pain tolerance" games. It wasn't a regular thing, in fact, it might have been just that once, but I do have a persistent and vivid memory of our eldest cousin pinching the skins on the backs of our hands (we three boys) between her long fingernails in our test of wills to see who would "break" first. Silly, perhaps, but are *you* willing to tolerate discomfort, sacrifice, lack, pain and the demands on both body and brain in the pursuit of your dreams? Perhaps it's time to renounce the "Cult of Constant Comfort"—the prime directive that says "if it's the slightest bit uncomfortable, I won't do it," that many people use to guide their decisions in life. Sometimes you just need to grow up, stop seeking the easy way out, stop whining, and "suck it up!"

> **Living Truism**: It is easier to tolerate inconvenience discomfort, sacrifice and pain when you stop being a child and become an adult.

A vital skill is... The ability to complete an action

Many people tell me they like working with me because I do what I say I will do. The ability to follow through, to complete a course of action and produce results is a skill not everyone has developed. However, if you intend to live true to your self, it is vital that *you* do. Creativity and the determination to produce are essential. Failure is not an option. Results are what matter.

> **Living Truism:** For many reasons—including the fact that unseen forces are called to bear when you are aligned with truth—it is easier to complete an action when what you do in life is in alignment with your purpose.

A vital personality trait is... Commitment

Dear Walt, My question to you is how do you maintain your motivation and excitement when you encounter frustrating obstacles? How do you remove the doubt as to whether this is the right direction, on those mornings when you wake up and the first thought that jumps into your mind is "Am I crazy?" You know what I mean? There are several of us that are out on our own...and we all struggle with that issue. ~ Doubtful in GA

The truth, dear Doubtful, is that there are no real doubts that I encounter, just minor detours and tests of my commitment. You see, I believe that every challenge has a solution, every destination has a path to it, and that the only way to find either one is to keep looking. I believe that my destiny is not in the hands of anyone but my creator and me, so I never doubt that I can accomplish my goals.

I learned many years ago the power of commitment. I learned it is possible and necessary to commit only once at the beginning of a journey. I learned that an obstacle is not my signal to question my commitment, but a chance to prove it.

Therefore, once I made the decision to walk away from my job and pursue my passion, the question became not "is this the right decision?", but "what do I need to do to make this happen?" In other words, I only ask "when?" not "if?"

The commitment was already made way back at the beginning. The ups and downs are just part of the journey. I can't tell you why I believe this, or what series of events in my life conspired to give me this perspective, but I know that it is what keeps me going forward even through the setbacks, evictions, credit challenges, etc., and everything I went and still go through during my journey.

But, as a result of your question, I started asking my self, "What is it that makes me this way?"

Maybe it's because I got encouragement at an early age for my academic accomplishments, and therefore don't believe there's any test I can't master if I work hard and smart enough.

Maybe it's because I'm prepared to fall without embarrassment. I gave up being controlled by how others judge me a long time ago. In fact, it's the first thing that needs to go if you're serious about becoming free.

Maybe it's because I'm a control freak who is fanatically driven to be in control of my life, and will settle for nothing less.

Maybe it's because I get physically sick if I have to work in an air-conditioned, corporate environment, and decided long ago that I wouldn't remain trapped in that world.

Maybe it's because I have a fear of mediocrity that won't allow me to settle for being an "also ran."

Maybe it's all these things, or none of them. I may never know the answer. What I *do* know is that once I stepped out on my own, going back was never an option. Giving up my ultimate goal of freedom was never an option. Neither is giving up the desire to help others do the same.

Remember, any decision made in the direction of experiencing your greater self, your happiness, and the fulfillment of your purpose and passion are never "wrong." They are all learning experiences and pathways that move you towards your ultimate destination.

If you are truly moving in the direction of your happiness, then those are not pangs of doubt you feel, but merely reminders that you need to be more resolved and creative in bringing your happiness to fruition. It should neither be the difficulty of the path nor the obstacles you encounter that determine the strength of your commitment. The ultimate realization of your dream is something that is entirely up to and within you. You must believe it's within your power to change the outcomes you've been creating, and give your self something different. [end "Ask Walt" response]

Yes, commitment (not the forced kind) is vital.

> **Living Truism**: It is easier to commit to something that (or someone who) offers you the option of freedom.

Non-attachment

A vital skill is...

To live true to my self, I practice a certain amount of non-attachment to things, outcomes, people and emotions.

Yes, I set goals and strive to reach them, but if things don't turn out exactly as I would like, I don't resist. I go with the flow, seek the silver lining, find the lesson to be learned, grow from the experience, and reset my expectations. I know the universe is perfect. I believe there is divine order at work.

Yes, I set standards of behavior, but if people don't behave exactly as I would like, I don't judge. I accept that people are here for different reasons, and are not obligated (or often, not even able) to act in certain ways simply because I expect them to. I go with the flow, file the lessons away for future reference, and reset my expectations.

Yes, I have possessions I value, but I also continually practice a philosophy of minimalism.

Yes, I strive to live in the moment and embrace the range of emotions that humans experience, but when catastrophes, disasters and accidents occur, I don't panic. I keep my wits about me, find the actions necessary, and take them calmly and efficiently. I believe and accept this unique and profound insight into the nature of things: stuff happens!

A vital personality trait is... **Focus**

The secret to success through all of life's chaos and turmoil is to stay focused on what's important, and not to waste time in worry. Many of us tend to worry about:
1. Things that have already happened.
2. Things we cannot control, that will likely never happen.
3. Things in the future, we don't know if they will happen.
4. Things in the present, which we can do something about.

It should be obvious that worrying over items 1 through 3 is a waste of time. It makes no sense to worry about a past you cannot change, events which may never happen, things you cannot control, or a future you cannot predict. Focus on four—things you can do something about.

A vital personality trait is... **Empathy**

The ability to see how others see

This is perhaps a *habit* based on a vocational skill set, or a *creative talent* more so than a personality trait. However, as a teacher, when I write, coach and consult, I have developed the ability to see the world the way others see it; to listen carefully to detect what is missing from another individual's map of the self, of other people and of the world, and fill in the blanks as necessary. I choose to do this because I am motivated by a personal mission to help others succeed. I am willing and able do this because I am not threatened by another's success.

> **Living Truism:** It is easier to empathize when you are not in competition, you believe there is enough for everyone, and you believe people generally do the best they can do.

A vital personality trait is... The ability to recognize flags

Some refer to them as "handwriting on the wall." A good friend and I refer to them as "yellow or red flags."

Particularly when it comes to interpersonal interactions and assessing an individual's character and compatibility, many people tend to ignore what are often telltale clues.

A friend of mine met a guy at a club, from the very first dance, she found that the way he "guided" her to the dance floor felt just slightly uncomfortable and controlling. He drove her home after the date, and on the way, stopped at his house to retrieve something he had forgotten, and locked her in the car while he went upstairs. I told her these were sure yellow flags.

I reminded her that when you first meet someone, that's when he or she is usually on their "best" behavior in order to impress you and make a good impression. So if this is who he is when he's *trying* to please you, imagine what things will be like later when he's *not* trying so hard.

She continued dating him, and sure enough, as things progressed, he became even more controlling and manipulative, and she ended the relationship.

The people you meet will always reveal their selves to you and tell you who they are, if you know what to look for, as well as the significance of what you find. The way they do one thing, is the way they do all things. Therefore, if you notice some troubling behavior, something that you have an instinctive gut reaction to, something that turns you off, don't overlook it. Respect your intuition; recognize it as the yellow (proceed with caution) or red (stop, turn and run for your life!) flag they are. Don't let desperation, delusion or daydreaming blind you to reality.

A vital personality trait is... **A sense of humor**

Two gerbils walk into a chiropractor's office....

A vital personality trait is... **Adaptability**

There's always a sorting or weeding-out process in effect in life. As unpleasant as it may be to accept, after all the chaos and turmoil has subsided, there will be some who make it through this weeding out, and some who will not. This weeding out of the old may occur at any moment in your journey to live true to your self, so be vigilant. If you are committed to living true to your self, then adaptation is what you should always be focused on.

Adaptability is the ongoing, ever-changing response to the ongoing, ever-changing conditions that arise in your ongoing, ever-changing quest to live true to your ongoing, ever-changing self. Each twist in the road may require a different strategy. Each obstacle along the way may require a different adaptation, and may also serve to weed you out. But fear not, the three things that every person has in his/her arsenal of responses to these changes, are commitment, perseverance and faith.

Regardless of what happens with each and every situation that faces us, adaptability is what will be required. Ask, *What are the things about this situation I have control over? How can I adapt to this situation? What, if anything, can I do to improve the situation? If I cannot improve it, how can I hang on until things improve on their own?*

If you cannot find a way to adapt, then perhaps you are the one being weeded out. Remember, there is a void being created by the weeding and sorting. This void must and will be filled. It will be filled by those who can adapt, and by those who can see or create opportunity. The question is: will it be filled by you or by someone else?

Remember, you always have a choice. If you choose to stick things out, then for heaven's sake, don't whine. Whining depresses others, steals your power, and is not the best use of your time and energy. Remember what I said about focus. Whining is worrying about "worry items" 1 through 3. "Focus on Four" and adapt!

> **Living Truism:** It is easier to adapt to any situation when you practice non-attachment.

A vital personality trait is... The mindset for change

In order to adapt, it is necessary to have the right mindset for dealing with change.

People are frightened by the prospect of change because they fear losing control, but that's because they've bought into the illusion they even *have* control. The truth, as we've learned, is that the only thing you have complete control over in this life is how you respond to the things you have no control over. You cannot control people, the situations they create, or anything else. You can only choose how you will respond to those people and situations.

Each person's response to change will be unique, based on what they want out of life (i.e. their goals) as well as what they perceive to be their assets and weaknesses. There is no right or wrong response. You are free to respond in any way you choose to anything that happens to you. What can be applied to and used effectively by everyone, however, is a mindset for change. Having the right mindset for change can help you anticipate, interpret, respond to, and weather the winds of change—and come out on top regardless of where and how the dust settles.

My personal mindset for dealing with change is based on a life philosophy that welcomes and embraces absolutely everything that happens to me as being "good." (The Universe is Perfect.) As I've said, we live in a supportive universe that bends to our desires to provide everything we ask for. What that means is that from the very moment you fix your focus on what you desire—money, fame, family, love, whatever—forces are brought to bear that proceed to bring those things to you. In light of this, the two greatest challenges people face are (1) having and maintaining their faith that what I've said is in fact true, and (2) recognizing, interpreting and responding appropriately to the subsequent sequence of events and new people that often appear in their lives.

In Part 3, I spoke about the "reconstruction crisis" that occurs whenever you create new goals for your life. Once you set goals, and particularly, if you write them down, focus on them, and visualize them as goals, people and situations show up in your life to bring those goals to you. At the same time, people and situations you no longer need in your life are stripped away to make way for the new. It's that stripping away —the deconstruction—that frightens people, makes them doubt their desires, and fall back into their former ways thereby resulting in failure. That breaking down of the old to make way for the new is a necessary part of dealing with change. For the reconstruction process to work, however, you must be flexible in your definition of your self as well as others, free from the fear of what people think about you, courageous enough to attempt new things, and committed enough to see them through despite challenges and obstacles.

Here's what I do. When presented with change, I ask my self, "Given that this situation exists or seems about to happen, how can this help me achieve my goals?" Obviously, unless I'm clear on what my goals are, then it becomes difficult to see how everything that happens to me can help me achieve them. Furthermore, unless I'm flexible in how I define my self, I may spend my time and energy railing against the change and attempting to force things back the way they were rather than adapting to the new environment. When you think about it, it's the only mindset that makes any sense to adopt. It accepts what is, and focuses on what can be.

> **Living Truism:** It is easier to maintain the mindset of change when you do not live in fear of the unexpected,
> when you have the discipline to persevere
> when you keep your eyes on the big picture
> when you know you can endure discomfort
> when you know setbacks come to be overcome,
> when you know you can complete the actions
> when you know you can adapt
> when you know most challenges are not fatal,

*It is not the strongest of the species that survive,
nor the most intelligent,
but the one most responsive to change.*
~ Charles Darwin

My summary of personality traits

Living true to my self requires certain personality traits, certain abilities, certain beliefs, and certain behavior including: discipline, the ability to delay gratification, a long time perspective, perseverance, endurance, tolerance for discomfort, the ability to complete an action, commitment, non-attachment, focus, empathy, the ability to recognize flags, adaptability, the mindset for change and the ability to incorporate them all with a sense of humor and the underlying belief that whatever happens….the universe is perfect!

Part SIX
Promptings

*"Now I practice getting silent
to hear the falling of a pin
Yes, I'm learning how to listen
to the still small voice within."*
~ "Excerpt from "The Promptings Come In Whispers"
Life Rhymes for the Passion Centered Life

Self talk

As a result of what I believe about my self, about others, about the universe, and as a result of the personality traits I endeavor to hone, there are certain ideas that I use either as mantra or momentary motivation to keep me on track and living true to my self. Of course, a comprehensive list of *all* the things I say to my self from moment to moment to stay motivated and committed and taking action would be infinite, so these are the highlights.

What I say to my self

I always remind my self... **"The Universe is perfect"**

Whenever I am confronted with a situation that appears to be a delay or a failure or disappointment, I immediately keep reminding my self: "the universe is perfect, the universe is perfect."

My blog "Jamaican in China" didn't win the Jamaica Blog Awards contest....but the universe is perfect: competing in it made me improve my blog, being featured on the JBA website gained me new fans and followers, and I can still add "Jamaica Blog Awards Finalist" to my site and to my list of accomplishments.

When I arrived on the island of Hainan, the bus conductress forgot to let me know when my desired stop approached, even after I reminded her two times to let me know when...but the universe is perfect: so, I decided to stay on the bus for the entire route, got to see the city center, made note of additional hotels and neighborhoods (which came in handy when I started to look for an apartment), shopping areas, and made note of a supermarket that ended up selling a vegan treat I now enjoy every day!

I'll no longer be writing my Saipan Tribune newspaper column....but the universe is perfect: I now have more time to devote to writing several new books, and focusing on enjoying my nomad journey with less obligations.

In each of these cases, it would be too easy to cry "foul!" claim "fix!" fume, or fight. However, as I told a friend of mine, "...well I wouldn't say I'm JUST as happy....I'd say I was *"content with, and accepting of the unfolding of the universe. When something like this happens, my trained, and now almost instinctive response is to look immediately for the hidden benefit, or unrecognized opportunity being offered, and turn my attention to moving upward and onward in spite of what others may interpret as a good or bad circumstance. My mantras are "the universe is perfect," and "all things work towards my good." (Makes me a lousy activist, I think)."*

I always remind my self... "You can't get it back"

On a morning like this one, when I'm lying in bed at 2:16am, and I have the choice between (a) enjoying a few more hours of sleep until dawn, or (b) getting up and working on a project that needs completing, I remind my self that once those hours have passed, that I can never get them back. That motivates me to take advantage of this valuable, irretrievable thing called time, to push the project forward even if just by a bit. I never regret it. It's how I completed this book.

I always remind my self... "Every little bit helps"

As a writer, completing and selling books is how I maintain my "true to my self lifestyle." So, on those days that I may not feel like writing, after I've pushed my self out of bed using *"You can't get it back,"* I'll do something simple. Even if the only thing I do is dot every "i" and cross every "t," every little bit helps. It's something that pushes things forward to completion, and is one less thing I'll need to do tomorrow.

I always remind my self ... **"No regrets"**

"Darn! I should have said something to her. Now the moment and the opportunity and the beauty that she is, are gone forever. Man, this feels even worse than the possible rejection I might have experienced by approaching her."

Yes, even worse than the rejection, is the unanswered "what if?" the lingering frustration, the scene replayed futilely a hundred times, and the maddening powerlessness of regret. It's happened enough times in the past, that these days, the moment I see an opportunity to act, I now instinctively launch into action with the mantra, "No regrets!"

I always ask my self... **"Don't you think Oprah was tested?"**

When all manner of trials and tribulations beset me, I invoke "The Oprah Rationalization," and remind my self that in order to reach greatness, she too was probably tested at every rung of the ladder of success. *"Was it all a piece of cake? Were there tests for Oprah? If you can't handle this test, then you're not ready for greatness.* (Insert your inspiration/role model/virtual mentor of choice (Ali, Bill Gates, et al.) here.

I always remind my self... **"I don't fear men"**

Attempts at intimidation by bill collectors, roadblocks to progress by ego-driven authority figures, even predators who walk the darkened streets at night... *"I fear not the threats and posturing of mortal men."* Furthermore, in the same mental or literal breath...

I always remind my self... **"None of this is fatal"**

"My electricity has been turned off due to non-payment. My phone service has been disconnected, too. There's an eviction notice on my apartment door even as men and men assume their posturing. But, you know what? None of this is fatal. I'll survive."

I always remind my self... **"This, too, shall pass"**

"In the same way that I look back now on all the tests and challenges I've endured in the past, so, too, shall I look back on these current challenges. This is giving me great stories for a book!"

I always remind my self **"I'm here to prove a point"**

"I'm here to show others what can be done. I'm here to prove what can be overcome. I'm here to dispel others' misperceptions and uproot some stereotypes. I'm here to teach. I'm here to share what I learn in the process, so that others may grow. I'm here to prove a point. Bring it on!"

What I DON'T say to my self
(or to anyone else)

I never say... ## Anything I don't want to be true

Someone asked me recently how I manage to keep such a positive attitude all the time-even through all the change, turmoil, chaos and upheaval. It's simply based on my underlying belief about the world:

We live in a creative universe. The foundation for any creation is the belief system. The tools of creation are thoughts and words. Therefore, it's simple. If you believe that your thoughts create your reality, and that your words have creative power, then it only makes sense that you strive to think and speak only in ways that create the reality you desire.

In other words, I say anything that I don't want to be true. I don't say things like, "I'm not good in math." I would say instead: I'm working on improving my math skills. I don't say "I'm too fat." I would say instead, "I'm working on losing weight.

"Okay, Walt, but people need to know the reality of their situations, don't they?"

"Sure, but they already do, because they are living it. What they *need* to know now is that they have the power to create a new reality if they choose to."

This mindset doesn't require that you avoid the reality of a situation. It simply suggests that you craft your statements about your self, others and the world in ways that inspire hope and possibilities rather than negativity and doom. You've got nothing to lose and everything to gain.

No matter how true you believe something to be, if it's negative, there's no need to actually say it out loud. No good can come of it. In fact, you can actually choose never to say anything unless it helps and supports another human being (including your self) in thinking, believing and performing at their best. (Remember the old maxim: If you can't say anything good, don't say anything at all.) Most people are not inspired to excel when they feel depressed and hopeless about their situation. People generally rise to the level of their potential based on a sense of hope.

There's no good argument that favors choosing doom and gloom over possibilities, unless your agenda is to depress people, or take away their power. The news media is trapped in a cycle of reporting negativity in order to survive. You, however, don't have to be.

Anything else that I don't say are just corollaries of this major rule. For example:

I never say.... **anything that is a "limiting absolute"**

If I believe that anything is possible, and that my words have power, then I must stay away from any pronouncements that limit those possibilities. I call them "limiting absolutes."

In everyday conversation, limiting absolutes generally start with the words "Everyone...", "No one...", "We all know that...." or "It's a fact that..." and go on to describe a belief system that the speaker believes is indisputable fact.

For example, *"No one is going to just give you money without wanting something in return..." "Everyone knows you must crawl before you walk..."*

Who says? These are nothing more than beliefs; limiting beliefs that stifle growth. The point is not to debate whether these are true or provable, The point is to endeavor to say things that allow other possibilities to exist so that I am not limited in my expectations of the outcome of a given situation.

True or not, I gain nothing positive by saying it. I might however, lose inspiration, create a self-fulfilling prophecy, lose the hope that spurs the innovation and creative thought that may get me out of that situation. I don't need to keep saying things that are nothing but dream killers.

I never say... anything that de-edifies or discourages

As a coach, but more so, simply as a friend, my job is to encourage those around me to achieve and succeed.

"So, you want to write a book about the mating habits of mosquitoes that you hope will be a bestseller? Great! Let's see how we could make that work!

I would never say, *"That's a bad idea."*

The important thing I recognize is that someone is getting excited about possibilities and it's important to sustain that spark, ignite the fire, fan the flame, and then guide her thinking to include more considerations, and eventually reach an idea with more potential. In the process of exploring the possibilities, and asking the right questions, she'll likely come up with that winning idea "on her own!"

Similarly, I'm careful not to pass judgment, paint in a negative light, criticize, expose as "bad," attack, shame, discredit, or otherwise de-edify someone in the presence or perception of another. I cannot build my self up by tearing others down.

I never say... Anything that gives away my power

Nor do I allow anyone I work with to do the same. People give away their power to many things in many ways. They do this in the way they speak and act in regard to life's possibilities. They give up before they even begin. They give their power to fate. They give their power to government. They give their power to perceptions of what other people think of them. Don't give away to an external entity or force outside of you the power you possess to steer your life. The reason people find it so hard to live true is that they've given away their power to belief systems that, in some cases, were specifically designed to rob them of their power. That keeps them dependent and controlled, and thus unhappy. Studies have shown that the degree of contentment in a person's life is directly related to how much control they feel they have. A greater sense of control equals greater happiness.

I never say... # The word "try"

Yoda was right. There is no "try." There is only "do" and "do not." Have you ever invited someone to a party, and they replied by saying, "I'll try and be there?" Did that person eventually show up? You'll find that more often than not they didn't (and will not). You see, the word *try* is actually an excuse for a lack of commitment. You promise to *try* to accomplish something when you are not committed to the outcome, but you're being polite enough to give your excuse in advance. That way, when you "fail" (as you already intended) to produce the promised result you can say, "I tried, I really tried…..but I just couldn't make it."

In my life, instead of "try," I say "I will," (or "I will not)", "I intend to," "this is what I plan to do," etc. Most people are simply not aware of the power they have within them. Let me illustrate.

Imagine someone said to you, "Meet me on the corner of Main street and Maple on the 15th January of *next year,* and I'll have a briefcase that will contain one million dollars in cash, free, clear and tax-exempt for you, and all you have to do is show up." Would you say, "I'll try and be there. I have to see what the baby-sitter is doing that night, and check my schedule?" Most likely not. You would say, "I WILL be there! It's done!" In fact, after waiting all year, and excitedly counting down the days on your calendar, you might even camp on Main and Maple from the night before, to be certain you don't miss your appointment!

Well, the truth is, you can bring that same level of excitement, certainty and commitment to anything you do, whether there's a million dollar payoff or not. If for no other reason, you can do it for the reward of being known as someone who is honest and upfront about your intentions, someone who keeps your word, delivers what you promise, and lives true to the self.

I never say... ## The word "problem"

Instead, I use the words *challenge, situation* or even *opportunity*. The word "problem" causes (often negative) flashbacks to math class—and may be something for which there is no solution. However, a "challenge" is something you rise to meet; a "situation" has no overt negative connotation; and an "opportunity" is something you eagerly pursue and mold to your benefit.

I never say... ## Anything that argues for my limitations

Sometimes, when I coach my clients, it seems *I* am more committed to their success than *they* are. I'll suggest a course of action towards a desired outcome, and they'll respond, "I could never do that. I'm just too shy," or "that would never work, because I (or someone else) tried it, and here's what happened." They argue why something *cannot* be accomplished. They argue on behalf of their limitations!

A wise business mentor once said: "The result of arguing on behalf of your limitations, is you get to keep them!"

I never say anything that is an argument in defense of the continued existence and possession of my limitations. There are enough people who will do that for me, as well as my potential. What my potential *really* needs is an advocate, someone to champion it and its ability to *overcome* limitations!

My summary of the promptings

However, beliefs, personality and self-talk, even working in concert, aren't the whole answer. They represent the foundation that supports the structure of my life, but are not enough to advance the momentum of the construction process, or sustain the long-term existence of what I build. For that I need an ongoing strategy of accomplishment, a construction schedule, as well as a maintenance plan—if you wish—a *process* for creating and sustaining the life lived true to self.

Part SEVEN

Process

"Action may not always bring happiness; but there is no happiness without action."
~ Benjamin Disraeli

What I do

The only way I—and others—know that I am living true to my self is that I am producing results—results that are consistent with my concept of living, my concept of truth, and my concept of my self. These include the tangible and visible manifestations of my choices—freedom from the rat race, books, products, passive income, the nomadpreneuring; it also includes the not-too-obvious results—the physical health, the peace of mind, the sense of fulfillment. I could not produce these results without a few secrets for the persistent, continuous actions that produce such results. This is what I do.

My Overall Strategy

- ☐ Align with purpose
- ☐ Set my targets
- ☐ Do something to make it real
- ☐ Walk, think, sit, stare
- ☐ Envision the future
- ☐ Seek synchronicity
- ☐ Rehearse outcomes
- ☐ Develop a strategy for execution
- ☐ Brainstorm, write it all down
- ☐ Work from lists
- ☐ Categorize, and Execute
- ☐ Find the critical path
- ☐ Overcome inertia
- ☐ Sustain the momentum
- ☐ Decipher clues
- ☐ Transform setbacks into opportunities
- ☐ Evolve as guided
- ☐ Complete the cycle of action
- ☐ Produce Results

Very important: Even though these items are presented in a linear checklist fashion, they are not strictly sequential steps. Typically, they are all happening at the same time. In fact, a better way to represent them, might be like this:

>   Evolve as guided
>   Transform setbacks into opportunities
>   Rehearse outcomes
>   truth   Develop a strategy Envision future
>   Make it real Set targets   Seek   Find critical path
>   synchronicity   Overcome
>   Brainstorm, write Align with purpose   inertia
>   Work from lists   Produce results
>   Walk, think, stare
>   Work from lists   Categorize execute
>   Sustain momentum   Complete cycle of action
>   Decipher
>   clues

What I do is... ## Align my self with my purpose

This part of the process actually precedes the goal setting. At this stage in my life, I don't even set goals that are inconsistent with my definition of living, my definition of truth, or my definition of my self.

Once you are clear about what living true to your self means to you, you'll know immediately if a suggested goal is in alignment with your purpose or not. Once you're clear on your purpose and your passion and your definitions, your goals and your purpose become one and the same.

A friend recently contacted me to join him in a lucrative business opportunity selling coffee. My answer was immediate and non-negotiable. I said, no thank you. Not because I was in China traveling. Not because it wasn't potentially lucrative. Not because I was too busy writing books. I said no because I don't drink coffee, and I believe it is harmful for the human body. I could not and would not consider such a business. It would be inconsistent with my personal belief system.

What I do is... ## Set my targets and goals

Setting goals is the most important part of managing your time. If your time is not being spent on activities that are related to your goals, you will end each day with an underlying feeling of frustration. I suggest to you that managing your time is really about ending the day with the feeling that you've not simply been productive, but that you've moved a step or two forward toward a worthy ideal or goal.

I use the Goal-Setting Template (see Appendix) to set the targets and goals for my project. I create my ideal scene which helps with my visualization.

What I do is... **Do something to make it real**

This is actually a proven technique for bringing your ideas into manifestation. Developers do it when they create a miniature, scaled model of the community they intend to build. Inventors do it when they create a prototype of their envisions invention. You should, too. One of the best ways to move a project or idea forward is to do something in the physical world to make it real. Create a prototype. Create a mock-up. Write and print an article about your self enjoying the realization of your goal as if you were profiling you for a famous magazine. . Focusing on the physical world is best, but anything that you can do to achieve a tangible, visible representation of your goal will help. For many of my new projects, the first thing I do is reserve a domain name, and start creating the website so I have something to sit and stare at.

What I do is... **Walk and think**

I do my best thinking when I pace, or when I'm standing.

What I do is... **Sit and stare**

Many are the hours I simply sit and stare at my website. Many are the hours I sit and stare at the manuscripts and rough drafts of my books. I often sit and stare at the covers of my books. I imagine that if I had a brick and mortar store, I would sit outside and stare at the frontage and awning and front door and window display of my store. I would probably walk around the store for hours staring at the products.

What I am (or would be) doing at those moments is pretending to be the customer. What are they going to notice first? What will be their impression? What image do I wish to convey? What is the best placement of this or that item, of that word, or that sign?

> **Living Truism**: No time or energy spent on thinking or acting (or even sitting and staring) to create your desired reality is ever wasted. Every little bit helps.

What I do is... **See the future**

This is an ongoing process. I never stop thinking about the manifestation of my goal. I am always brainstorming. I am always seeing the end result.

What I do is... **Seek the synchronicity**

I see how it all fits in, and what other things are happening that portend a good outcome. I find other projects (mine as well as other people's) that create synergy, note world events that might indicate I'm on the right track.

What I do is... **Rehearse outcomes**

This helps me to develop my Plan B, or several of them. In broad terms, for any wish desired, there will either be a yes, or a no outcome. By rehearsing the situation, I prepare my self for either outcome, and then develop a series and sequence of responses to each possibility. I do this for everything in my personal as well as business life.

Let's say that tomorrow I am going to visit a vendor to negotiate a deal. Since people will do what people will do, I ask my self, "What if he doesn't agree? What if I simply don't like the vibe I get from him? What will I do then? What are my other options?" There are always other options in life. Rehearsing the outcomes helps me see them.

My response to life may be defined as *"the instantaneous affirmative reframing of setbacks, coupled with the never-ending contemplation of other options."*

What I do is... **Develop a strategy for execution**

I begin each new project by implementing something called the Non-Existence Formula. This is a powerful formula I learned in a Scientology course that can be used for anyone beginning a new venture, job, role or position.
1. Find the lines of communication
2. Make yourself known.
3. Discover what is needed or wanted.
4. Produce or deliver.

If the project is ongoing, I implement the appropriate Condition formula. *[See Turn Your Passion Into Profit]*

What I do is... **Brainstorm all conceivable angles**

Finding the lines of communication for a new book project for instance, requires brainstorming about all the possible places the book could be seen, sold, reviewed, profiled, excerpted, etc. In my brainstorms, I include milestones, goals, strategies, creative ideas, "wouldn't it be nice ifs," things I'd like to do, and everything that comes to mind as it relates to my project.

What I do is... **Never let a thought pass me by**

This tip, buried 184 pages into this book, may, in fact, be the most important secret for living true to your self.

Once the brainstorming starts, it never ends. On a bus, in a dream, washing the dishes—at any moment in my day, an idea in the form of an impulse, a flash of clarity, a hunch, can come to me that is actually an important step on the critical path to take me quickly to me goal. It could be a thought to read a particular book, an idea for a product, a letter to write, an email to send, a "what if" scenario that comes to me as I brainstorm, a related wish that I'd like to see fulfilled.

How do I know if it's connected? It doesn't matter if I can see the connection or not. Everything is connected. If I've already started brainstorming and rehearsing and envisioning my ideal life, then it probably is connected in a profound way. Here's what I do: I WRITE IT DOWN. NEVER LET A THOUGHT PASS ME BY. I stop whatever I am doing, find a pen, or laptop and write down the idea on my continuing "master list." (Yes, I'll even interrupt my shower for this.)

I don't need to see where and how it fits into the overall scheme of things right now. The goal is to get it down on paper so that it exists in a tangible, retrievable form. Once I do this, a few things usually happen:
- Other related ideas will come along (I write those, too)
- Things will start to manifest. (There is an unseen realm)

By doing this, I am creating an on-going, ever-evolving master list of things to do, things I'd like to see, possibilities, ideas, goals which becomes my master "to do" list. My continuing mission, which I continuously get better at over time, is to translate each thought into an action item that can move me toward my goal.

What I do is... **Categorize the list**

I find that a good brainstorm will include items that fall into several categories: (a) creative ideas, (b) research, (c) marketing/publicity, (d) sales, (e) milestones/goals. I've also found that when I'm deciding on what to spend my time actually executing, that I tend to focus on developing new creative ideas (my favorite) and so, have to be careful that I don't jump from one idea to the next without doing the necessary research, marketing and selling to launch the idea, generate income and continue living true to my self.

What I do is... ## Avoid the flawed plan

Any plan that relies too heavily or solely on the actions of another individual, an outside force, another person's whim, goodwill or largess in order to be successful, is inherently a flawed plan. It may provide a short-term stopgap measure, but there is no dependable future or control built in. Therefore, you must *always have a 'Plan B.'* What will you do, and more importantly, what are you putting in place now just in case your "Plan A" falls through? One sure way to live true to your self at all times is to never allow any one person or situation to hold the key to your success or happiness.

It makes more sense to have a Plan B when you understand that nine out of ten people will drop the ball not out of malicious intent or even incompetence, but simply by virtue of being focused on their own agendas.

What I do is... ## Execute, using my secret weapon

I have a "secret weapon," a secret time management weapon I've been using, and which has served me well since 1989 when I discovered its magical powers. I've used it to run my passion-centered business while I still had a day job. I used it to match my salary and quit my job to become a full-time *passionpreneur*. I've since used it to launch dozens of websites, write twenty books, hundreds of articles and accomplish quite a lot. Want to know what it is? The secret weapon I use to manage my time and be so productive is a simple 6" x 9" hardcover, ruled notebook. Yep, that's it. But it's really what I do *inside* that notebook that holds the key.

I've read that all great achievers work from lists. So, to be a great achieve, I too, start each day by composing a list of the things that I need to do to move me toward my goals. This list also includes my daily task and errands.

If my goal is to write a new book on business startups, my list of items in my notebook for today might look like this:

[] Wed, Dec 19
- *draft table of contents*
- *write chapter 1*
- *apply for ISBN number*
- *interview business owner A, B, & C*
- *search the Internet for related titles*
and will also include items that might not be related to my
      immediate goal
- *deposit check at bank*
- *pick up soap, fruits at grocery*
- *respond to John about new website idea*
- *email schools re: Career Day essay contest*
- *clean up junk in closet*

    This habit of working from lists is magical. I find it makes my life and my time much more manageable and productive in a number of ways. First, writing your ideas and tasks down on paper frees your mind of the burden of having to remember every little thing that needs to be done on a given day or for a given project. Writing your goals and tasks impresses them into your subconscious mind and activates unseen forces to mobilize to bring you the people and circumstances necessary for their completion. Writing your goals and tasks on a regular basis gives you the opportunity to review them continuously throughout the day so you can assess what is doable, what is important, what is urgent, and what is irrelevant. Save these notebooks, and they will provide you with a record of your activity, a process you can use again for the next project, contact information, and insights into your thought processes over the years.

    I make a commitment to my self that I will not do anything today that is not on my list. Of course, if something occurs that is really urgent, I will have to focus on it, but what I always do *first* is write it down. So, if while I'm drafting my table of contents for my book, I get an email or a call from John requesting a response, I take a minute to add "respond to John" to my daily task list, and then keep working.

    Work on the essential. Whenever you have a free moment, especially after completing a task, simply open up your notebook, scan your list and ask your self: "What is the best use of my time at this very moment?" or you might ask, "If I were called away on a three-day trip today, what are the three items on this list that absolutely could not wait until I return?" or "which activities will move me forward toward my goal(s)?" Get in the habit of doing only those things that are directly related to your goals. Some items may not be related to my book, but are time-sensitive (i.e. notifying schools of Career day contest), and need to be done right away. Some items might be desirable, but not on the critical path toward completing my book (i.e. clean up junk in closet; apply for ISBN number), and can wait until a later date.

As I complete an item on my task list, I place a check next to it on the left side. At the end of each day (and this is important), I transfer all the incomplete items to my list of tasks for the next day, on a brand new page of my notebook, along with any new items that come to mind as I write. In addition, if, as I scan the list, I realize that something I had written yesterday is not that essential after all, then I simply omit it from the next days' lists.

I've found, over the years, that this amazing tool and technique for managing time helps me accomplish in one year what others need five years to do! And as powerful as it is, it represents only twenty percent of the secret to successful time management. The other eighty percent, often lies in what I know, not what I do.

What I do is... **Develop a "To Know" list**

Many years ago, I read *A Return to Love* by Marianne Williamson, in which she states something akin to "whenever we are stuck in life, many of us think there is something we need to do. There is, perhaps more importantly, something we simply need to know." The concepts in some books stay with you for a lifetime. This was one of those.

The reason most of us get stuck in life is because we harbor belief systems that limit our potential and our success. We spend our time worrying needlessly, obsessing over things we cannot change and fears that aren't real.

What's troubling you at this very moment? Are you worried about paying bills? Are you afraid you won't find a partner to share your life? Are you in debt? Are business sales down? Whatever the issue, it likely stems from fears and misperceptions that are crippling you. At times like these, what you know may be more valuable than what you do.

Introducing the 'To Know' List?

As an entrepreneur living true to my self, my "To Do" list is often quite lengthy, with web sites to update, e-mails to send, books to edit, columns to write, coaching sessions to conduct, interviews to grant, and so on. Sometimes, however, my list gets longer and longer, but the amount of forward motion and progress I seem to be achieving gets less and less. Sales decrease, visits to Web sites fall off, and I feel like I'm spinning my wheels—stuck. At those times I invoke a strategy inspired by Marianne's words. Instead of a "To Do" list, I make a "To Know" list.

A "To Know" list is a list of truths that dispel fears. For every fear and misperception that paralyzes or distracts you, there is a corresponding truth that, if you believed it, would set you free. It might amaze you what you can accomplish seemingly by doing nothing at all and simply reminding your self of truths you should know and live by.

My private 'To Know' list

So, I share the actual "To Know" list I used this week to get unstuck. (Some have been omitted in the interest of modesty. After I wrote them, I dropped the "I need to know that" part and simply used the rest as affirmations.)

I need to know that there is abundance.
I need to know that the universe is perfect.
I need to know that I am enough.
I need to know that my good is already here.
I need to know that I am protected.
I need to know that every battle need not be fought.
I need to know that often there is nothing to do but be thankful.
I need to know the right apartment will come at the right time.
I need to know that money always comes to me.

Are you struggling with debt and scarcity? Then perhaps you need to know that there is always abundance.

Are you feeling in the midst of chaos and uncertainty? Then perhaps you need to know that the universe is perfect.

Are you feeling inadequate? Then perhaps you need to know that you are enough.

The transformative truths about our true nature, reality and the universe can be gotten from any number of self-help, spiritual and inspirational texts. Seek them out.

Act like you know

So, how would your life be different if you believed and knew these truths? How would you feel and act if, in the midst of chaos and uncertainty, you knew that things would work out because the universe is perfect? How would you feel and act if, in the middle of your loneliness, you had the absolute confidence that you would meet the perfect person at the right time? How would you feel and act if, in the midst of a slump in sales, you knew that abundance was your birthright? You would probably spend your time doing any number of other more positive and productive things rather than worrying about what may or may not happen. You would walk and talk fearlessly and confidently through life-which has the effect of attracting equally fearless and confident situations and people into your life, thus fulfilling the prophecy, as it were.

For any given obstacle, fear or negative emotion, there is always at least one lesson (i.e. something you need to know) that is holding you back. I had a situation recently that had been gnawing at me for several days. I experienced an encounter with someone that left me feeling slighted. I felt I needed to counter tit for tat with a little show of power of my own. At the same time, I knew that that desire for justice, that urge to assert my self, beat him at his own game, and "win" this little confrontation was just my ego talking. Still, I stewed in it for several days until I "got" that I was being tested.

I remembered that whenever I'm feeling nervous, angry, cheated, or unjustly dealt with, that there's something I needed to know. So I sat down and started writing my "To Know" list. I asked my self what lesson I was being taught, and remembered some words of wisdom a salesman once taught me: "When your ego is up, your income is down." I found the answer I needed. In dealing with this perceived slight, I knew that my greatest good and personal growth would only be served by remaining above the fray and simply walking away. I accepted that any justice that needed to be exacted in this situation was not mine to dispense, and I took the high road.

Amazingly, within minutes-mere minutes-of choosing the high road, and suppressing my ego, a flurry of events started happening. Sales picked up. Web site visits increased. I found the perfect apartment I'd been looking for-all within 24 hours! Coincidence? Not a chance. Not in *my* reality!

From woe to wow

Footnote: It wasn't until I shifted my focus from lack to abundance and started looking for evidence of it, that I realized that during the month of July, I had actually sold more books through Amazon.com than during any month on record! Since Amazon won't pay for July sales until 30 days later, all I was seeing was the net effect of all the expenditures on my account balance, while being totally oblivious to the abundance I was actually experiencing. Ahhh, the things a refocused mind will finally see! (i.e., my good was already there!)

The moral of the story

Having done all that I could do in the way of physical action, frantic activity, and ego-based considerations, I shifted to mental action, silence and a knowingness of certain truths, and my path was made clear. *I leave room for the unseen.*

So, my suggestion to you is to spend some time working on your own "To Know" list. Start by writing down how you're feeling. Then using my "To Know" list as a model, remind your self of the truths (simply the desired reality or high road beliefs) that would set you free. Really get into the feeling of it, then think, speak and act as if you really believed and knew these truths, and see what happens. The results might surprise you!

What I do is... Find the critical path

In moving forward to create an uncommon life, it is often necessary to separate unconnected events by finding what's called the "critical path." That's a term I learned during my career as a civil engineer working with construction project managers. Once I explain what I mean by this, it will likely seem quite simple on the surface. However, it's my experience that the inability to isolate the critical path, and more importantly, act out of sequence is what prevents people from realizing the successes they wish to. Now that doesn't mean you have to be trained as a project manager in order to live true to your self, it just means you have to know a little secret about how they think. Let me explain with a very simple example.

Let's say you're building a house. Many people would (1) lay the foundation. (2) build the floor, (3) construct the walls, then (4) build the roof, as their sequence of steps.

But what if you were pressed for time? Would it occur to you that you could build the roof *while* the foundation is being laid, and then simply hoist and lower the roof onto the walls? In fact, since the roof is "unconnected" to the existence of the walls, you could actually build the roof *first*?

The critical path in a project is the sequence of steps that *must* occur in a particular sequence in order to move a project forward. For example, you physically *cannot* install the windows until the walls exist. So building the walls is on the critical path. It is critical to the completion of the project. However, *constructing* or purchasing the windows is unconnected, and could be done at any time before the walls actually exist. Does that make sense?

In other words, many people think in a linear fashion, and believe action "A" must occur, before they can execute action "B." However, in many situations and projects, there are alternatives to that safe, intuitive, traditional sequence of steps.

Now, in general term, here's how I use this ability to live true to my self. Often, when I was just starting out, desperate to make the sale or the secure the project, I would promise to produce a result, hoping that an item on the critical path of producing that result would come occur in time for me to be successful. I might promise the client "C," so as not to lose the sale, while having no idea how I was going to provide "A" and "B." I can do this because:
1. I believe that multiple alternatives always exist
2. I have faith in my ability to find these alternate solutions
3. I am prepared for the consequences (to lose the sale) if I can't

And, in addition, as you now know about me, I believe I am special, I believe I can do the impossible, I believe there's a knowable formula for everything, and, perhaps most critically, I believe in miracles and magic!

What I do is... **Eat raw**

I would say my diet is about 70% raw, uncooked fruits, vegetables and nuts and may vary based on what's available where I may be living. The other 30% consists of cooked grains (brown rice, millet, quinoa), as well as some vegan, non-dairy packaged treats (cereal, food bars) that I've grown accustomed to. When I do cook, I follow the suggestions contained in the book, *Ideal Meals* by Sasha Poznyak, in which, for example, I learned I could boost my brain function simply by eating longan fruit and rambutan, and ended up writing three books—including this one—simultaneously!

What I do is... **Fast**

Another thing I do to increase creativity is fast. Sometimes I fast by default, since I get so consumed in what I'm doing that I have little desire for food. Other times, I may deliberately fast for a few days in order to cleanse my system. I find that those times often coincide with a new project, so I seek the synchronicity.

By fasting, I mean not eating any solid foods for several days. I may do a water fast, or a "lemonade fast" (lemons, maple syrup, cayenne pepper, spring water; Search online for *The Master Cleanser* by Stanley Burroughs]

Fasting also helps to reaffirm and hone the discipline I believe is critical to producing results.

What I do is... **Create more time as necessary**

You've no doubt heard all your life that there are only 24 hours in a day, but there's a way to create more hours than your daily allotment: find your passion. You'll find that people can manufacture time for the things that are important to them.

Have you ever noticed that when you are engaged in a hobby or activity you find enjoyable that time just slips by and two, three, ore more hours can pass that feel like only one? Have you also noticed that what you accomplish in that time is also quite impressive? When you are engaged in an activity or pursuit that is in alignment with your purpose and passion, you enter a timeless zone in which you are more efficient, faster, more inspired, more confident, stronger and more productive. Your mind and body receive instructions from unseen places that help you make the necessary connections, take the right actions, make the right choices, and do the best "next thing" to move you efficiently toward completion. That's where the additional hours needed for great achievement come from. You too can rise to the level of your greatest potential when engaged in the thing *you* came here to earth to do. Get in the zone. Your goals, and therefore the items on your daily list should be related to your passion and purpose.

What I do is... ## Get in the zone

Writing is a critical part of living true to my self. When the time comes to get creative, I have few strategies, tools, techniques and things I've discovered about my self that help me get in the zone to be most effective.

I work best in the mornings between 2:00 and 6:00am.

I need to be away from people.

Music is my mantra. I put the song, "Light My Way" by U2, on in my headphones and use it to zone in and away. (Beginning at point 3:50, the song's chorus, and my mantra, *"baby, baby, baby, light my way"* begins and repeats over and over. I've written several books, including this one, with that hypnotic chorus playing in my ears. (Over a span of six years, that song has played 1038 times, while the next most played song, "Released" by Glenn Philips, has played 446 times.)

What I do is... ## Decipher clues

If I believe the universe is perfect, and that all things work towards my success, then I need to seek out, recognize, identify, interpret, process, then apply and/or respond to the clues that are always being offered by a supportive universe.

What I do is... ## Act immediately

Once I separate unconnected events, find the critical path, decipher a clue or intuit the next step to take, I move with all possible speed to act quickly. This is essential because (1) sometimes an opportunity is time-sensitive, (2) doing one thing clears the way for another thing to fill the void, (3) after taking a step, I arrive in a different place, the view changes, and what is required changes, too. I can't delay too long before acting, and I can't plan too far in advance with any degree of specificity, because the view will constantly change.

What I do is... **Plan spontaneously**

An oxymoron to be sure, and an idea that may seem a bit at odds with having a long time perspective, but the truth is, I do not have ten-year plan, or a five-year plan. In fact, I'm not even sure where I'll be next week. I have only a long-range vision of where I am going, and what I wish it to look like. In a similar vein, I don't even rehearse or write detailed outlines for my presentations or speeches. A few minutes before any negotiation, talk or presentation, I simply remind my self, *"I always say the right thing. I always do the right thing."* That, essentially, is my spontaneous plan.

And throughout all of this ongoing, evolving process...

What I do is... **Coach my self as needed**

I remind my self, *"The universe is perfect, Oprah was tested, this too shall pass, I am here to prove a point, etc."*

What I do is... **Inspire my self as required**

Sometimes I take an inspiration interlude and listen to motivational recordings or watch the life stories—the rise from obscurity to prominence—of Bob Marley, Muhammad Ali or The Beatles. (Don't tell anyone, but I also watch the movie, *Scarface,* for the same motivation.) I recently discovered and watch old episodes of *Inside the Actors Studio,* a television series that features interviews with actors and performers who talk about their life stories and the perfection of their craft.

What I do is... **Reward my self as necessary**

As I've said, I consider a life lived true to be its own reward. However, upon a completing a project or achieving a particular milestone, I'll reward my self with an experience I've been delaying, an acquisition that's been on my list, or some overpriced vegan treat and eat my self into oblivion!

What I do is... ## Connect with the earth as mandated

It occurred to me recently that as a consequence of living in the concrete jungles of the world, there are actually people who live their entire lives without actually touching the earth. Think about it. They are born in a sanitized, concrete hospital. They are carried into and transported in a car that is touches asphalt. They live their lives in high-rise apartments, and walk to school on cement sidewalks. They travel to work in steel trains. They live their entire lives, eating, sleeping, and every waking moment separated from the earth hundreds of feet above the ground. And if, on that infrequent occasion, seek natural settings that are free of concrete or asphalt cover, they wear socks and slippers and sandals and shoes that separate them from the actual living earth. And, to take a few steps back in time, remember, they were even conceived and began the very instant of life in the womb of a woman who, similarly may never have touched the physical earth.

What effect do you think that might have on the world view, thought processes, bodily functions, and even basic humanity of an individual, a family or society to have essentially a nation of people who have never touched ground —people who are not, you might say, "grounded?"

In electrical terms, to ground an object means just that, to connect it to the earth. This is done because as an electrical appliance operates, for instance, it will build up an electrical charge. The earth naturally attracts excess electrical charge into itself and dissipates it so that it does not accumulate and cause harm to the user. *You ground something to keep it functioning properly and so it doesn't cause harm to itself or to others.* I'll let you ponder, the significance of that statement.

What I do to ground my self is head to the beach and walk barefoot in the sand, or climb a mountain to a secret location, strip naked, lie directly on the rocks and bake my self in the sun. Are you grounded?

What I do is... ## Sustain it all

I'll invoke a few analogies to make an important point.

Living true to my self is like driving a car on a journey. It's easier once the car is moving and has achieved momentum. But if I am not vigilant, if I do not keep my eyes on the road, my destination in mind, my foot on the gas pedal, and my hand on the steering wheel, it can drift, run off the road into a ditch or, worse, crash and end the journey.

Living true to my self is like living in a house. It's easier once the structure exists and I reside there, but if I do not maintain it, fix the leaks, repair what becomes broken, replace what gets worn out, paint the walls, shore up the foundation, it will deteriorate, fall into disrepair and eventually cease to provide the shelter, the protection, and the lifestyle I desire.

Living true to my self is like flying a plane. It's easier once I've plotted my course, taken off, and ascended above the drag of the lower atmosphere, but if I do not navigate correctly, constantly readjust my course, adjust for turbulence, employ the laws of flight and propulsion and aerodynamics to remain in the air, I could drift of course, stall or plummet.

It is necessary, therefore, to constantly create and recreate what it means to live true to my self. I must sustain the image of my self and who I am. I must evolve as necessary. I must write new books. I must improve my marketing. I must never allow the vision of who I am and who I wish to be to slip from my awareness and control. To live true to my self, I must create the creating anew every day.

> **Living Truism:** To live true to your self, you must be vigilant and create the creating anew every day.

Summary of PROCESS

Living true to my self is the life-long implementation of my beliefs, thoughts and actions.

a FINAL WORD

"Life has come a long way since yesterday, I say
And it's not the same old thing over again, I say
Just do what you feel and don't you fool yourself, I say
'Cause I can't make you happy unless I am"
~ Ziggy Marley, *True to Myself*

Harnessing my neuroses
The Faith in Familiar Fears

Many years ago, when I was first beginning my personal development journey, it was a dear friend and mentor, Christie, who encouraged me to take the Lifespring™ experiential learning/personal growth course. She claimed that it would help resolve the issues that were causing me distress and feelings of being stuck that I was experiencing at that time. She also suggested I get a therapist.

I was reluctant. The armchair psychologist I was, believed at the time—and still do to some extent—that a certain amount of my fanaticism, drive, motivation and insatiable need to stand out, impress and excel were all rooted in a neurotic need to please, based perhaps on a deep inferiority and fear that I just was not good enough. And even though I recognized that having a sense of inferiority was a "bad" thing, I was proud of the accomplishments, the accolades and attention that such excellence brought. If that drive to achieve was based on neuroses, then I wanted those neuroses left intact. I *needed* them. They were my familiar fears.

If you're here on this plane with the rest of us, it means that you, too, may have some specific and familiar fears driving your life. I know *I* certainly do. Here are two of mine:

Fear of mediocrity
I have a deep-seated fear of mediocrity, of just being average, and I harbor a desire to be an overachiever. Being above-average matters to me.

Fear of confinement
I know, also, that freedom is very important to me. Not just the freedom of working for my self, or the freedom to travel, or to live where I want to live, but the literal physical freedom of unrestricted motion. One of my greatest fears—a phobia, if you will—is to be trapped, pinned down, restricted

such that I am out of control and cannot move. There's a scene in Quentin Tarantino's movie, *Kill Bill*, where "The Bride," the character played by Uma Thurman, is buried alive, locked in a wooden coffin with only about six inches of space between her and the sides of the coffin. When I even think of being confined like that, a panic response wells up inside me.

Whether this is due to some past life trauma, DNA memory or "just one of those things," I know that the need to be free, to not be confined—that I've extrapolated into my lifestyle in many ways—runs deep. Being free matters to me.

Releasing the Brakes

As far as I could tell at the time, my neuroses—these and other deep-seated needs—were helping me to excel in things that mattered! I excelled in school. I got awards. I received recognition. I got into a good college. How on earth would I survive and succeed without them???

Christie assured me, however, that I had it all wrong. I was not excelling *because* of the neuroses, I was excelling *despite* them. The neuroses were actually like the emergency brakes on a car that were engaged and holding me back while I was attempting to move forward. Once the brakes were disengaged, I would be able to accomplish *more not less*! I didn't buy it at first, but eventually, I relented, took her advice and embarked on a lifelong journey that included Lifespring™ as well as other self-help courses, books and workshops.

Perhaps you, too, feel attached to your neuroses, and that, to some degree, you are functioning adequately, perhaps exceptionally, in life as a result of them. Maybe you're driven by some nameless or named fear, some phobia, some focus, and some neurosis that you're attached to—that you've used to define your self, that represents a crutch you think you need in order to function according to society's paradigm. I'm going to suggest to you, as Christie suggested to me, that you, too, pursue the healing path. Your neuroses are not the source of your power, talent, drive or motivation. They are actually what are holding you back from living true to your self.

I never did find a therapist, so perhaps I'm still driven by those same neurotic needs I had back in college! However, assuming that all the years of focus on personal growth worked to some degree, and that I'm a less neurotic, less emotionally obstructed, less restricted, freer-thinking individual now, then I don't believe I would be here today, had I not taken Christie's advice and pursued the healing path. I *have* grown. I *have* changed. There are so many things about how I once viewed others, the world and my self that are part of my past. That pervasive sense of frustration is gone. I no longer feel trapped and stuck. And, guess what? I'm still achieving. I've found my purpose in life. I am helping others. I'm free of corporate confinement, and best of all, I'm living true to my self.

The bigger picture

The power of one life lived true

As quiet as it is being kept, the world is evolving towards a higher state of vibration—a higher state of consciousness and spiritual awareness. Those who control the "news," and who feed off the energy of negative, lower-level emotions won't report it, but all around the planet, people are awakening to new ways of thought and new ways of being. The youth are awakening to the flaws of their parents' generation. Societies are rejecting a misdirected capitalist imperative that sacrifices the beauty, and sustainability of the planet. Communities are rejecting multi-national corporations' control of the seeds they need for growing their own crops. Villages are protesting government and corporate control of access to clean water. Individuals are asking different questions of their selves in the quest for meaning and survival. Protests and demonstrations against the old world order abound. The veil is being lifted. Again, you can't find full and truthful evidence and reporting of this in mainstream media, but it is happening.

To assist in this global awakening and transformation, there are those who are choosing, and/or are being sent to different places for the purpose of raising the vibrational energy across the planet.

Think about it like this. Say you had a pot of cold water on a stove, and you added to it a single drop of hot water. There would be a small, barely measurable, but definite increase in the temperature of that pot of cold water. Eventually, if you kept adding more and more drops of hot water, the overall temperature of the pot would increase. The energy of that single drop of hot water, as well as each successive drop of hot water affects the overall temperature (i.e. vibrational energy) of the water in the pot. And so it is with YOUR presence in any community in which you reside. You may not be able to measure it at first, but your very presence in a relationship, in a family, in a group, in a community, in a village, in a city, in a country, and on the planet, affects the energy level of the whole. You are making a difference whether you realize it or not. There is a "butterfly effect*" that your thoughts and your actions have on the rest of the planet.

Therefore, your decision to live true to your self does, indeed, have consequences, repercussions, effects and impact in the larger scheme of things. Trust that it does.

*butterfly effect: the idea, used in chaos theory, that a very small difference in the initial state of a physical system can make a significant difference to the state of that system at some later time [from the theory that a butterfly flapping its wings in one part of the world might create tiny changes in the atmosphere that ultimately alter the course of, prevent or cause a hurricane in another part of the world](sort of like a domino effect)

My Final Summary
Find what drives you, and make it matter

So there you have it: my answer to the almost unanswerable question of how I did it. You now know what I did. You know what I believe, what I say to my self, what I never say, and what I do and don't do. You know what drives me, and what moves me to action. You also know, perhaps most importantly, why it is important for me to live true to my self. Freedom matters to me. It matters *enough*.

You've read this book all the way through. Perhaps, then, you're just like I am. Perhaps there is something that compels you to want to reinvent your self. Perhaps you feel the urge to actualize more of who you know your self to be. Perhaps there is something that drives you the same way freedom drives me.

I can't tell you what that thing is that drives you. Furthermore, if you already know what it is, I can't make it matter *enough* to move you to action. I can't make it matter enough to drive your self to the extremes that may be required for you to live true to your self. You will have to discover your own compelling reasons. Only you can make it matter enough. Only you have the power to discipline your self, to find and adopt the necessary belief system, to develop the right mindset, to hone the required skills, think the appropriate thoughts, say the right things, take the called-for actions, implement the strategies, and persevere until you achieve your dream.

My best advice to you, therefore, is to get clear about what that thing is. Make it matter. Then use any information, inspiration or ideas you've been able to find in my words to:

Re-claim your power!
Break free!
Live true to your self!

My heart is with you.

Any more questions?

My Guarantee

Living True to Your Self comes with a guarantee:

I can't guarantee you the race will be won
or that you'll always stay ahead of the pack
But the race never ends for the one who endures
so rest assured, you can always bounce back

I can't guarantee you the market won't dip
or your stock won't take a turn for the worse
But good plans for investing: sell short and buy long
and make blessings from what others call curse

I can't guarantee you we'll always be friends
or we'll always see things eye to eye
So just savor the good and hold memories in heart
even if the time comes for saying goodbye

I can't guarantee that they'll always look up
or your pedestal won't tip and then tumble
But *respect* is immune to life's rises and falls
for the person who lives true and humble

I can't guarantee you that power persists
unlike Rome, things can *fall* in a day
But lucky's the man who from pieces rebuilds
for to misfortune he never falls prey

I can't guarantee you there'll never be pain
or that your heart won't break if you fall
But I do know it's better to love fully and lose
than half-hearted or never at all

No there's no guarantee that you won't come up short
when you strive to live true to your plans
But you learn, laugh and love on the safe side of the fall
where control's squarely back in your hands

APPENDIX

"Teachers open the door. You enter by yourself."
~ Chinese Proverb

Kybalion summary
Achieving Goals
Goal-Achieving Template, Sample
Goal-Achieving Sample
About the author
Coming soon: Living true to your EGO

Kybalion summary

I. THE PRINCIPLE OF MENTALISM.
   "THE ALL is MIND; The Universe is Mental."

This Principle embodies the truth that "All is Mind." It explains that THE ALL (which is the Substantial Reality underlying all the outward manifestations and appearances which we know under the terms of "The Material Universe"; the "Phenomena of Life"; "Matter"; "Energy"; and, in short, all that is apparent to our material senses) is SPIRIT,

II. THE PRINCIPLE OF CORRESPONDENCE.
   "As above, so below; as below so above."

This Principle embodies the truth that there is always a correspondence between the laws and phenomena of the various planes of Being and Life.

III. THE PRINCIPLE OF VIBRATION.
   "Nothing rests; everything moves; everything vibrates."

This Principle embodies the truth that "everything is in motion"; "everything vibrates"; "nothing is at rest"; facts which Modern Science endorses, and which each new scientific discovery tends to verify.

IV. THE PRINCIPLE OF POLARITY.
   "Everything is Dual; everything has poles; everything has its pair of opposites; like and unlike are the same; opposites are identical in nature, but different in degree; extremes meet; all truths are but half-truths; all paradoxes may be reconciled."

This Principle embodies the truth that "everything is dual"; "everything has two poles"; "everything has its pair of opposites."

V. THE PRINCIPLE OF RHYTHM.

"Everything flows, out and in; everything has its tides; all things rise and fall; the pendulum-swing manifests in everything; the measure of the swing to the right is the measure of the swing to the left; rhythm compensates."

This Principle embodies the truth that in everything there is manifested a measured motion, to and fro; a flow and inflow; a swing backward and forward; a pendulum-like movement; a tide-like ebb and flow; a high-tide and low-tide; between the two poles in accordance with the Principle of Polarity.

VI. THE PRINCIPLE OF CAUSE AND EFFECT.

"Every Cause has its Effect; every Effect has its Cause; everything happens according to Law; Chance is but a name for Law not recognized; there are many planes of causation, but nothing escapes the Law."

This Principle embodies the fact that there is a Cause for every Effect; an Effect from every Cause. It explains: "Everything Happens according to Law"; that nothing ever "merely happens"; there is no such thing as Chance; while there are various planes of Cause and Effect, the higher dominating the lower planes, nothing ever entirely escapes the Law.

VII. THE PRINCIPLE OF GENDER.

"Gender is in everything; everything has its Masculine and Feminine Principles Gender; manifests on all planes."

This Principle embodies the truth that there is GENDER manifested in everything — the Masculine and Feminine Principles ever at work. This is true not only of the Physical Plane, but of the Mental and even the Spiritual Planes. On the Physical Plane, the Principle manifests as sex, on the higher planes it takes higher forms, but the Principle is ever the same. No creation, physical, mental or spiritual, is possible without this Principle.

Achieving Goals

The achievement of one's goals, no matter how large or small the endeavor, relies on goals, purposes and activities being aligned and organized.

A goal is not something one decides upon which then miraculously comes to fruition, just because one decided it would. The attainment of a goal necessitates that certain actions be carried out in the real world which effect some change for the better and a step closer toward its accomplishment.

One can be working toward a goal, but discover that his actions do not yield any forward progress. This occurs not only for an individual in his life, but also for an organization, state or country of any size. This can be a result of the plans, actions and other factors not being aligned to attain the goal.

There are actually a number of subjects that make up any activity. Each of these must operate in a coordinated manner to achieve success in the intended accomplishment of the envisioned goal.

GOALS: A goal is a known objective toward which actions are directed with the purpose of achieving that end.

PURPOSES: A purpose is a lesser goal applying to specific activities or subjects. It often expresses future intentions.

POLICY: Policy consists of the operational rules or guides for the organization which are not subject to change.

PLANS: A plan is a short-range broad intention thought up for the handling of a broad area to remedy it or expand it, or to obstruct or impede an opposition to expansion.

PROGRAMS: A program is a series of steps in sequence to carry out a plan.

PROJECTS: A project is a sequence of steps written to carry out one step of a program.

ORDERS: An order is a verbal or written direction to carry out a program step or apply general policy.

IDEAL SCENES: An ideal scene expresses what a scene or area ought to be. If one has not envisioned an ideal scene with which to compare the existing scene, he will not be able to recognize departures from it.

STATISTIC: A statistic is a number or amount compared to an earlier number or amount of the same thing. Statistics refer to the quantity of work done or the value of it.

FINAL PRODUCTS: A valuable final product is a product that can be exchanged for the services or goods of the society.

(Excerpt from Targets And Goals by L. Ron Hubbard)

Goal Achieving Template

The following is a goal-achieving template you can use for any goal.

MAJOR Program:

Situation: _____

Purpose: _____

Major Target: (broad general ambition)
1. My broad general ambition is to....

Primary Targets: (organizational, personnel, communication steps)
1. _____
2. _____
3. _____

Vital Targets: (essential for operation at all)
1. _____
2. _____
3. _____

Conditional Targets: (gather data about if, where and how a project can be done, then go into action)
1. _____
2. _____
3. _____

Operating Targets: (directions, actions, schedule or timetable)
1. _____
2. _____
3. _____

Production Targets: (set quantities for statistics)
1. _____
2. _____
3. _____

Valuable Final Product & Ideal Scene
My valuable final product is _____
Ideal Scene: In my ideal scene: _____

Goal Achieving Template Sample

Here is a sample of how I might use the template to achieve the goal of increased exposure and sales my own product.

GOAL: increase sales of *Living True To Your Self* book.

SITUATION: All the advanced reviews and feedback so far indicate that this is a unique book that many people would find insightful, informative and entertaining. There is tremendous untapped potential here. I want to achieve massive sales and global reach for the book and its concept.

PURPOSE: Establish my self nationally as a self-help writer, and best-selling author; increase sales of this and all my products, improve my standard of living, and achieve even higher levels of financial independence and reach.

STRATEGIC PLAN: The plan is to use my existing channels as well as my existing reputation and nomadpreneur accomplishments to market the book.
- Offer free *Living True to Your Self* previews, articles and excerpts
- Promote to my existing mailing lists and social networks
- Target press release to media
- Conduct tele-classes and workshops once book is released
- Target book clubs; speaker associations; mlm companies/gurus
- Target to schools, continuing education institutions

Major Target: (broad general ambition)
    1. To increase national attention for my book
    2. To achieve sales of 100 copies per day
    3. To increase overall sales of all my books

Primary Targets: (organizational, personnel & communication)
    1. Set up Team Tour, Media friends and Gatekeepers
    2. Hire translators as necessary

Vital Targets: (essential for operation at all)
1. Keep websites up and running at all times
2. Maintain cash flow and cash-on-hand
3. Have media kit and video ready and available
4. Ensure that print-on-demand manufacturing is in place

Conditional Targets: (gather data about if, where and how a project can be done, then take action)
1. Find out daily sales required for Amazon Top 10
2. Find out the hot topics for magazines/tv/radio

Operating Targets: (directions, actions, schedule or timetable)
(PROMOTE via Press Releases, Articles, Ads, Workshops)
1. Set up new title with Manufacture
2. Contact Entrepreneur Magazine again re: writing articles
3. Advertise on various career sites
4. Advertise in Selfgrowth.com newsletter
5. Send copy to Oprah Show & Magazine
6. Use PR service to distribute press release
7. Create magazine query; submit to inflight magazines

Ideal Scene:

In my ideal scene, thousands of people each week purchase the book through Amazon and/or through my own website. My inbox is flooded with "Notification of Payment Received" emails every day! My bank account grows from daily deposits. Orders are fulfilled quickly and customers return to the site frequently. In my ideal scene, visitors to my site number in the thousands daily. They order books and e-books and other products. Using my philosophy and formula, a living true movement is created. The book is an Amazon as well as a New York Times bestseller. It has been translated into 20 languages. I receive invitations from around the world to read and discuss it with fans. Book clubs use my books to spark interesting debates. Other life coaches and career counselors use it in their own practices. It has become the hottest new thing in inspiration and self-help. People are talking about it everywhere!

~ END OF SAMPLE ~

Coming soon? **Living True to Your EGO**

by Walt F.J. Goodridge

ego [ee-goh] *–noun*
1. The self, especially as distinct from the world and other selves.
2. In psychoanalysis, the division of the psyche that is conscious, most immediately controls thought and behavior, experiences and reacts to the outside world, and is most in touch with external reality.

If I were to live true to the definitions above, as well as to purists of Psychology terminology, the title of this book should, in fact, be *Living True to Your Ego*. It's actually a very intriguing title, and were it not for the fact that I had already completed the entire living true to the self philosophy, with the word "self" so interwoven into the fabric of the philosophy, I might have used it.

An expert offered me some insights: *"An advanced Ego function is typified by finding the most comfortable, enriching, and independently sustainable environment for ones' desired affairs, while not infringing on those of others, as, naturally, that would produce counteraction by the other, and jeopardize one's comfort. The Self, however, is far from being concerned about comfort, and in fact a lot of self-exploration will lead to a colossal discomfort. Having a healthy Ego function is an integral attribute of emotional maturity....*

Once we speak of the ego, however, we invoke all manner of distinctions and definitions (Jungian, psychoanalytical, etc.) that tend to complicate the simple premised on which this book is based. There is also the subtle negative connotation that surrounds the word ego, as it is commonly used when referring to someone as "egotistical" or having a "big ego." To keep things simpler, therefore, the title of the book shall remain as is, and while I'm ever-so-intrigued by the marketing potential of the "ego title," I'll have to relegate my curiosity about what might have been, to alternate realities, concurrent timelines, and parallel universes, and simply speculate on what might have been!

Other books from Walt

NEW FREEBIES SINCE THE PANDEMIC!

The Pandemicpreneur Report
How to Make Money in this New Global Paradigm ...Without Ever Leaving Your Home!

    A guide for choosing the right product, platform, profit & promotion strategies to generate pandemic-proof income.
- The Pandemicpreneur Toolbox
- 7 business-building strategies
- A Rough & Ready Business Plan
- A Master Checklist for getting started
- Links to resources, tools & apps
- Lessons from the past & predictions for the future
- The 23 Laws of Pandemicpreneur Success

The Zero Cost Business Operations Manual

"For every product or service offered for a price on the Internet, there exists a comparable or better alternative offered free!"--Goodridge's Second Law of Internet Economics

    Discover all the zero cost (or dirt cheap) resources, tools, services, software and apps I personally use to write and design and publish my books, make videos and courses, create websites, succeed at Search Engine Optimization, run every aspect of daily operation and generate location-free income–for $0 or very close to it!

The Ageless Adept's Master Shopping List, Substitution Checklist & Immunity Top 10!

    What do I, the Ageless Adept, buy when going grocery shopping? What's in my spice rack? What healthy condiments do I keep on hand? What kind of juicer did I get? Want to see my colloidal silver generator? Yes, I have a coffee grinder (for enemas only, of course!)

Find "FREE" items at www.waltgoodridge.com/store

The Passion Profit™ Series

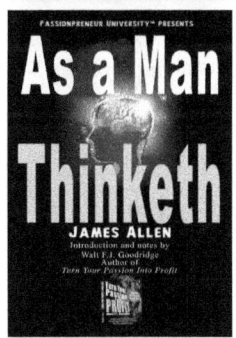

Facebook.com/passionprophet
Youtube.com/passionprophet
Website: www.passionprofit.com; **Blog**: www.passionpreneur.com

Find "FREE" items at www.waltgoodridge.com/store

The Hip Hop Entrepreneur™ Series

  Facebook.com/hiphopentrepreneur
Website: *www.hiphopentrepreneur.com*

The Jamaican Nomad series

  Facebook.com/jamaicaninchina
Youtube.com/jamaicaninchina
Blog: *www.jamaicaninchina.com*

History We Write™ series

 Facebook.com/historywewrite
Website: *www.historywewrite.com*
   Find all "FREE" items at www.waltgoodridge.com/store

Living True to Your Self   217

The Ageless Adept™ Series

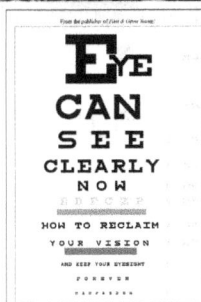

Facebook.com/agelessadept
Youtube.com/agelessadept
Web: www.agelessadept.com **Blog**: www.agelessadept.com/blog

Discover Saipan™ Series:

Facebook.com/welovesaipan
Youtube.com/discoversaipan

Find all "FREE" items at www.waltgoodridge.com/store

Living True to Your Self   219

Blogs by the Author

The Passionpreneur Blog: *"Follow my lead with tips to help you turn your passion into profit and make money doing what you love!"* www.passionpreneur.com/blog

The DiscoverSaipan Blog: *"Discover the history and the mystery of this unique piece of the US located in the western Pacific"* www.discoversaipan.com/blog

The Jamaican in China Blog: *"My adventures in the Asia-Pacific region as a single, nomadic, vegan cheapskate!"* www.jamaicaninchina.com

The Ageless Adept Blog: *"How I Live a Natural Life in an Unnatural World!" Includes the new REVITALADE™* www.agelessadept.com/blog

Youtube Channels by the Author

The PassionProphet
www.youtube.com/passionprophet

The Ageless Adept
www.youtube.com/agelessadept

Discover Saipan
www.youtube.com/discoversaipan

The Jamaican in China...and Beyond
www.youtube.com/jamaicaninchina

*****

About the Author

Walt F.J. Goodridge is from the Caribbean island of Jamaica and holds a Bachelor of Science in Civil Engineering from Columbia University in New York. After seven years working for the Port Authority of New York & New Jersey, this frustrated civil engineer walked away from his career to pursue his passion for writing and helping others. His mission: *"I share what I know, so that others may grow!"*

In addition to identities as the "Hip Hop Entrepreneur author," "the Jamaican in China," and the "Ageless Adept," Walt is known as the "Passion Prophet," author of *Turn Your Passion Into Profit*, and a unique PassionProfit™ Philosophy & Formula.

Walt escaped from America to live on the Pacific island of Saipan, Commonwealth of the Northern Mariana Islands (CNMI), and has written several books about his new home: *Saipan Living, Doing Business on Saipan, Chicken Feathers & Garlic Skin, Saipan Now & There's Something About Saipan* and others.

He writes freelance articles for the *Saipan Tribune, Marianas Variety* and *Guam Business Journal;* conducts writer workshops to help aspiring authors; offers tours of the island; has been featured in books and documentaries about the islands; received a Senate Resolution for his contributions to CNMI society; and received Governor's Humanities Awards for (1) Preservation of CNMI History, (2) Research & Publications in the Humanities, and (3) Outstanding Humanities Teacher.

The Wall Street Journal, Entrepreneur Magazine, Source, Billboard, Time, Black Enterprise, Essence, Ebony, South Africa's SArie Magazine and authors including "Guerrilla Marketing" guru Jay Conrad Levinson, and music industry pioneer Chuck D, have featured, quoted or endorsed his work. His books have been used as texts for university courses in the US and Europe. Walt currently owns and operates over 50 websites, has written well over 25 books, 400+ business articles and 500+ "life rhymes."

He lives an untethered, minimalist, vegan, nomadic lifestyle, but responds to emails to walt@passionprofit.com! Download Walt's CV & Media Kit at www.waltgoodridge.com

www.ingramcontent.com/pod-product-compliance
Lightning Source LLC
Chambersburg PA
CBHW060151050426
42446CB00013B/2776